Managing Remote Teams

How to achieve together, when everybody is working from home

Lukasz Szyrmer

Managing Remote Teams

How to achieve together, when everybody is working from home

Lukasz Szyrmer

No part of this book may be reproduced in any form or by any mechanical means, including information storage and retrieval systems without permission in writing from the publisher, except by a reviewer who may quote passages in a review. All images, logos, quotes, and trademarks included in this book are subject to use according to trademark and copyright laws of the United Kingdom.

© 2020-2022 Launch Tomorrow

Tweet This Book!

Please help Lukasz Szyrmer by spreading the word about this book on Twitter!

The suggested hashtag for this book is #ManagingRemoteTeams.

Find out what other people are saying about the book by clicking on this link to search for this hashtag on Twitter:

#ManagingRemoteTeams

Managing Remote Teams: How to Achieve Together, When Everyone is Working from Home, 5th edition
Published by LAUNCH TOMORROW
Warsaw, Poland

Copyright 2020-2022 by LUKASZ SZYRMER. All rights reserved by LUKASZ SZYRMER and LAUNCH TOMORROW.

No part of this book may be reproduced in any form or by any mechanical means, including information storage and retrieval systems, without permission in writing from the publisher/author, except by a reviewer who may quote passages in a review. All images, logos, quotes, and trademarks included in this book are subject to use according to trademark and copyright laws of the Poland.

SZYRMER, LUKASZ, Author
MANAGING REMOTE TEAMS
LUKASZ SZYRMER

ISBN: 978-1-7397977-3-7
BUSINESS & ECONOMICS / Business Communication / Meeting & Presentations
BUSINESS & ECONOMICS / Organizational Behavior
SELF-HELP / Communication & Social Skills

QUANTITY PURCHASES: Schools, companies, and groups may qualify for special terms in bulk. For information, email bulkpurchase@managingremoteteams.co.

Contents

Introduction 1

Rethinking meetings 13

Quick challenge ideas 15

Why rethink meetings when going online 17

The impact of "Where" we meet online 23

Who needs to be involved 33

How to contextualize when remote 45

How to run successful meetings 59

How to move meetings online successfully ... 81

Top 15 tips when running your meetings online 91

What you can do now 99

Section takeaways 107

Rethinking motivation 109

Quick challenge ideas 111

Why alignment is linked with motivation 113

How to reduce ambiguity and why it matters . . 123

Forests, trees, and motivation 135

Why context drives people 149

Why department boundaries matter most 167

How to align or realign within a company 175

If the direct approach fails 193

How to break down silos in your company 209

What you can do now 217

Section takeaways 235

Rethinking productivity . . . 237

Quick challenge ideas 239

So how do we know our people are working? . . 241

Why traditional productivity measures don't add up 247

What we've got here is a failure to delegate . . . 251

The wolf you feed 263

Given outcomes, teams can manage their own work 279

How to apply a team lens to output 289

Revisiting individual productivity 301

How to track productivity in real-time 305

When will the team be *done*? 319

What you can do now 325

Section takeaways .335

Epilogue 337

Appendices 339

Principles, quotes, and rules of thumb 341

Glossary. 343

Bibliography. 347

Resources 351

Introduction

Exploring an alternative way to achieve together-through others, who are all remote.

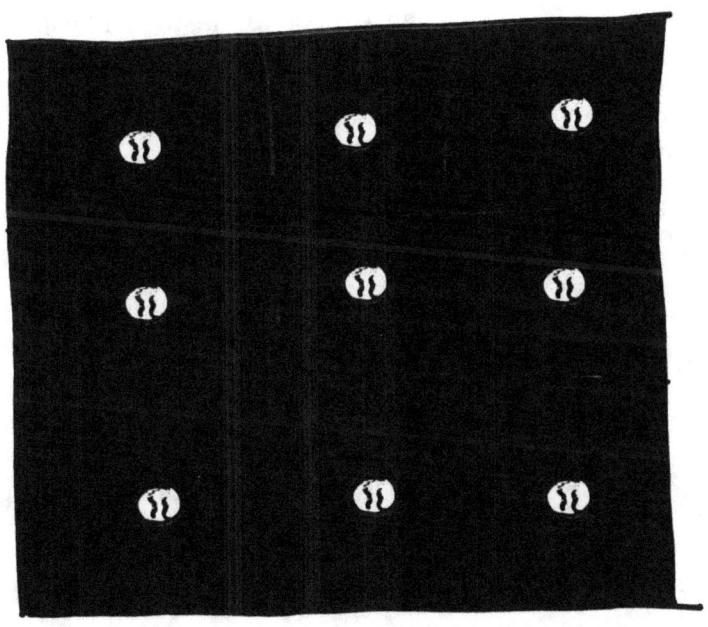

"So glad to see everyone on the call"

Work is fundamentally a social experience. Just ask any professional parent who tried to work from home with small kids during the pandemic. As adults, we need each other to decide what is important, what finishing work ultimately means, and finally...to actually do the work. To collaborate effectively, we each need to understand what our co-collaborators want: their intent. If we don't see it, we guess. We 'fill in the gaps', based on our communication with them. And the meaning can be easily misconstrued. For example, 'We're done' sent in a text or chat message can imply a brutish end of long-running romance. Or completing a major milestone like a new product release. It depends on who's saying it and what has happened leading up to that message. Instead of taking a look at what makes remote work unique, this book examines what has stayed the same: how our relationships at work and the wiring of our brains help us define and achieve what's meaningful-together.

Who am I to be talking about this?

My name is Luke Szyrmer. I've worked and managed remotely over a decade to date. I've successfully led teams spanning multiple continents, time zones, and industries. I've seen what works and what doesn't, in large companies and in fast growing startups. While I respect the value of rigorous testing in academic research, I'm a classic practitioner. I only care about theories that explain what's going on, and that produce results in practice. This book started as an experiment, to solve specific problems I faced, with proven ideas I could try to apply with my teams. A lot of them weren't useful or relevant, but this book contains the ones that are.

When the pandemic hit, lots of online content about remote working appeared, although much of it included lists of "37 tools to help you work remotely" for example. It was well-meaning, but written by desk researchers who had as much remote experience as their readers.

Looking at the impressive volume of activity around remote work, I also found very little advice specifically for managers. After the initial shock died down, CEOs shared big visions around the future of work in their industry and their company. The rank-and-file employees figured out a way to make do with ergonomic keyboards and standing desks. But the average middle manager was still on the hook to ship and make things happen in this brave new world, without the ability to work with and through others based on body language and other in-person cues they traditionally relied on to guide them.

Two years have passed. We've navigated the downs and ups of remote culture shock. While our context changed dramatically to fully remote, our brains remained the same. The overnight change, and how we coped, revealed a lot about working together with others. We've started to come up with better ways of working together. We are now ready to consider what truly matters, what is truly important about remote work: how humans collaborate and achieve together. Let's use technology as an enabler, and not an inconvenience by default. And to achieve together effectively, regardless of where we work.

* * *

Despite being a member of Generation X, I was lucky enough to grow up as a 'digital native'. In truth, I was that kid. The kid who handed in school papers printed on a dot-matrix printer and written on a word processor, when everyone else hand wrote their homework. My dad brought home a series of desktop computers from work. I played games, tinkered with them, and swapped stories with friends about how to get the most out of the latest soundcard. At the time, each computer was self-contained, located physically in one place.

I started college in 1994, just as the internet started connecting computers and their owners into a global network. I was among the lucky pioneers ever to collaborate digitally with people–without meeting them in person for years. Thanks to a few eager professors, the English department maintained class-specific 'listservs', and invited students to class-specific online discussions. These were early open source equivalents of what was later commercialized as Google Groups for example (now itself a dinosaur in Internet years). You sent an email to an alias, and that alias resent your email to everyone else. Technically it wasn't that complicated, but interpersonally-broadcasting an email to strangers raised awkward concerns.

- Who would read it?

- Do I know then?
- What would they think if they don't see me?
- What if no one responds? what does that mean?

It was like a bad Seinfeld episode of seemingly meaningless social questions, all which were critical to establishing and understanding the sender's relationship with the group members. By engaging in email discussions with strangers, we'd establish a baseline for how the group would interact later. Little details served to replace body language. You worked out the intent of a message based on that context, similar to how body language worked in person. You 'filled in the gaps'.

Meeting without a meeting.

This is a good example of the nuance to meetings. In meetings, we decide what matters and what we're going to do as a group. Just because most business meetings are poorly designed, that doesn't imply that meetings themselves are worthless. Just try excluding someone from a meeting. Or canceling all meetings for a team. I speak from experience. You'll hear more about that later.

One thing is for sure: getting 'remote' right requires you to be a lot smarter about meetings that you organize and participate in.

* * *

When I finally landed my first job out of college–as a self-motivated, self-taught programmer no less–I'd been assigned to work with a few engineers based out of Switzerland. We were building a new embedded software platform for big ticket vending machines…techy even by my standards today.

It was an ambitious technology platform redesign, funded by an unsuspecting US East Coast public transport network as the first client to get it. There was a lot of ambiguity in what the customer needed, like regulatory constraints. For example, one train stop at a small village existed solely because a powerful state senator lived there. Of course, it also had different fare structures, routing logic. The requirements document alone was over 500 pages. 50% of it was out of date at any given time, but nobody agreed which 50% it was. By the time it was updated, something else was out of date. The whole project was rife with uncertainty.

The best way to build systems like this is to model the customer's understanding, and reflect it in the structure of the system. If requirements change later, it tends to be much easier to adjust the internals of a system built this way. But the Swiss engineers decided they would build the core of the platform in a fancy programming language in Berne, assuming that the US satellite office would write scripts to customize the platform. In short, they circumvented my boss and the customer completely.

Paradoxically, they chose to build a core system themselves, leaving the client-specific scraps for remote offices like mine. From the perspective of a technical career, they used and learned skills in a powerful and valuable programming language. My colleagues and I were expected to tweak their solution in a non-transferrable language. I was disappointed. In my frustration, I started arguing my case using the same long email style. They were full of witty and punchy sentences worthy of an ex-English major, or at least so I'd hoped.

One of the Bern-based software architects found my emails to be too 'forward' and presumptive. In their view, my American writing style and overeagerness weren't convincing. Just annoying. Eventually, my boss realized he had to send me to Switzerland in order to shake out our differences in person.

That first meeting in the office has been hard to forget, even though it happened over twenty years ago now. Sun coming in through the office bay windows on my left. Jens, the lead Swiss architect, sitting cramped over his keyboard. I walk up to him to introduce myself sheepishly. He acknowledges my presence, looking up. He gets up, offers his hand while looking slightly away. I remember that initial lack of eye contact still today.

Over the week, we eventually had a few conversations during my stay. But the decision was made earlier. Not feeling heard and included, I started looking for a new job. And left the company a few months later, after we'd released the product we'd just finished.

Having gotten that job based on sheer self-motivation to learn about technology, I learned on my own skin how alignment affected my own motivation to be part of a team. On one hand, a motivated maniac eventually does really well in this line of work. The ability to learn was more important than the technical skills that were typically screened for. On the other hand, it was easy to lose an employee, even someone highly motivated, to misalignment–across teams in this case.

At this company, the problems were many and unclear. The agenda wasn't framed properly. There were too many competing priorities, and as a result, we were constantly distracted. Geographic location only made the work harder. It forced us to communicate digitally. This meant we'd have to 'fill in the gaps' which mattered when there were differences and ambiguities to iron out.

From a remote leadership perspective, we didn't know what was important overall and to our teams. We ended up fighting amongst ourselves more than necessary, in order to set those priorities. And while this can happen with everyone working in one office together, when you're partially or fully remote, the strife and confusion feels greater–has more emotional impact because you're 'filling in the gaps'.

*   *   *

Fast forward a few years. I was working with a close knit financial technology team in a London-based office. We had a decent rhythm on a team of four. Then our tester dropped a bombshell. She announced that she was leaving to join former colleagues–at a different company. After a big release, we were allocated a remote tester in the Riga office, who we'd never met physically. How would this work? We were used to convening around a bunch of stickies and physically moving them around as we knocked off tasks. It clearly couldn't work physically any more.

Bit by bit, we worked out how we could hand over work to each other across time zones. We 'met' each other virtually, finding out about one another. And surprisingly after about a month or two, we'd pretty much returned to the high pace of work we were accustomed to previously. We just fell into a pattern that really 'flew'.

When the tester flew over to meet us in person months later, we already felt like we knew a lot about one another. We'd 'filled in the gaps', and created a working relationship that worked. Worked so well, in fact, that I replicated it in future roles, and even managed to scale it up a few times.

As I advanced to coordinate the work of a team and later of multiple teams, that experience served me well. At the peak, I ran 3 teams across 13 time zones and 9 locations, a mix of in office and remote. It was possible to do the highly creative and technical work of software development remotely. While it certainly was convenient to be in an office, it wasn't necessary.

In short, I know remote leaders can achieve high levels of group creativity when collaborating remotely. I've done it before multiple times. You can, too. Coming to the office was truly optional. While it was admittedly awkward starting new relationships without meeting someone in person, given enough time it didn't matter. How we worked and collaborated mattered a lot more than where we were physically.

* * *

Humans have a need to 'fill in the gaps', to make sense of what others want based on what they communicate to us. There is a greater gap when we work digitally, but ultimately it's a distraction. Even for types of work that require individual focus, craft, and 'deep work', like programming or writing for example, the value of that work will partially be determined by other people and the meaning they attach to it. Whether it's important.

This book goes into three different aspects leaders must really understand when running remote teams, in order to lead effectively:

1. rethinking meetings
2. rethinking motivation
3. rethinking productivity

Even though it's a bit cliche in IT circles, you need to go back to leadership first principles in a remote context. Figure out how they apply in order to help teams achieve consistently in this new environment. Without first principles, you end up stuck trying to recreate 2019. At this point, it's safe to say that we will never go back to 2019. Even if you try to recreate it in your company, there are thousands of alternatives that employees have if they want to work remotely.

In other words, while I am writing about collaboration, ultimately the question is how to lead effectively regardless of your team and your own location.

Let's dig in, shall we?

Rethinking meetings

In which we focus on where the action is and ensure that everyone can execute effectively

"Now that we all agree, let's get on slack to discuss why it will never work at our company."

Quick challenge ideas

The fastest way to learn something new is "learning by doing". To introduce change to your teams, you need to start by trying something new yourself to figure out what might work.

The following are specific things you can try, to figure out if there might be a better way for you and your team to work. Put the book aside, and try doing one of these before you continue reading:

- If scheduling a meeting, schedule it for twice as much time as needed. At the beginning of the meeting, suggest that you might not need all of the scheduled time. If you finish early, you'll have that time to catch up on non-meeting work or just recharge.
- Send an email suggesting a no meetings day policy for one day per week for your team. Trial it for a month. I like Wednesday, personally.
- If you already use an online whiteboard, try running the whole meeting using the pen/pencil tool. Minimize the use of text. Draw your agenda as a pie chart. Draw options other people propose as you listen. And so on.
- If someone says they haven't had the time to prepare for a meeting, give everyone 10 minutes to prep during the meeting. For example, if you've prepared

a report, give everyone time to read it before you discuss it.
- If you have a data connection and the weather is nice, grab your phone, make sure you have your company's meeting app installed, and take a walking meeting. Or work on your chat app as you walk.
- If you have your company's meeting app installed on your phone, work for an hour or an entire day from your phone only. Feel free to walk around the house, lay down, etc.

The aim here is to step slightly outside of your current routine(s). It might feel somewhat uncomfortable, but you'll realize you have more autonomy than you assume.

Feel free to email me with any observations at customer-success@managingremoteteams.co.

Why rethink meetings when going online

To say the least, I was taken aback. I was noticing a pattern of silence in calls, even though we'd just returned from a productive in-person workshop with the whole team.

One day, an operational standup call had over-run to about twice the scheduled length. During the call, my boss, an architect, and I were metaphorically "pulling teeth". No one wanted to say anything. The architect even explicitly referenced the teacher played by Ben Stein in the 80s movie Ferris Bueller's Day Off saying, "Anyone? Anyone?"

an old meme

Immediately after we hung up with the team, I called my boss to do a quick post-game analysis.

"You see what I mean, here, when I said they don't seem involved," I started.

"I don't get it," he said. "They aren't saying anything unless we ask them directly. We pay them, and it's part of their job to participate in meetings."

My stomach tightened.

"I think we're missing something here, but I don't know what it is."

It wasn't a team quality issue. The team was composed of people who were probably the best in the company. I had a lot of respect for each individual's expertise from when I worked alongside them in the trenches. They were locking up exactly when they could contribute the most to the conversation and decisions. And I was pretty sure they were keen to be part of it. The new product initiative was started with a lot of fanfare. And to be honest, it was already almost an honor to be part of the team.

"But I don't think it's a question of pay or anything formal," I continued. I had a team of 14 allocated full-time to this initiative. It's not like anyone was pulling them off to different priorities. "It's almost like they are just really distracted, and this distraction even shows up during meetings. And presumably, it's the same thing throughout the day. Or maybe they were afraid to speak up."

I couldn't fall back on peeping to see what people had on

their monitors, which worked for in-person workspaces. All I had to go on was what I saw happening. And what I heard during meetings. The intuitive mirroring of others' emotional states didn't work online. Feeling connection through physical touch, like a handshake bolstered with oxytocin, wasn't there anymore. Granted, I was only meeting with the team as a whole for a small part of the week due to time zone constraints.

This was primarily about going remote. The human dynamic fell flat. It caught me off guard, and I didn't realize how big of a task I had ahead of me. Instead of lacking empathy, I was overwhelmed. In the words of Erica Dhawan, author of *Digital Body Language*, I "didn't know what empathy meant anymore in a world where digital communication had made once-clear signals, cues, and norms almost unintelligible". If non-verbal communication in person makes up 90% of what we communicate, and only 10% is about the content of the message, then we are missing the building blocks of connection: posture, proximity, smiles, pauses, yawns, tone, facial expressions, and volume or losing it depending on the speed of our internet connection. For example, one research study found that with intermittent delays of 1.2 seconds, people were more likely to be rated as less attentive, friendly, and self-disciplined than if there was no delay.

Skip rethinking meeting dynamics at your own risk. Offices become less important, even if they are distributed. And meetings and company culture are woven into people's personal lives and vice versa. All participants' experience of meetings changes significantly in that case. This is true regardless of the symptoms you are seeing:

- A lack of engagement
- A company culture that doesn't support change
- An inability to finish things

Meetings are the first and easiest place to start diagnosis. They are practical and specific. Everyone is there anyway and sees what happens. This is particularly true for recurring meetings.

If you can fix one meeting, the positive impact accrues over many future months of work. For this reason, recurring meetings have a highly leveraged impact on productivity: a good one pulls it up a lot, and a bad one can drag it down. While they are not a "silver bullet" that magically makes all of your problems disappear, getting your meetings right means it's easier to make decisions together and hold everyone accountable for them. With solid meetings, it's a lot easier to dive deeper into motivation, productivity, and several other factors.

And once I improved online meetings after a lot of experimentation, the team came together. I didn't need to organize meetings myself anymore; they were happy to convene without me if needed, but included me when they wanted my input. Team members supported one another. They owned the work they picked up. And with all of that working correctly, it made it possible to go after more ambitious goals.

Before moving on to the how-to details, let's dig into why this worked for me in the following chapters.

Key takeaways

- When moving online, meetings change significantly because of how we read body language and tone of voice.
- Be prepared to rethink meetings from the ground up, to get them to work for you, your teams, and your company.

The impact of "Where" we meet online

When I was organizing an offsite for a team that seemed to be coming together after some struggle, I needed to get the flight details from everyone. Eighteen different people were flying into the target location from multiple airports and time zones. My boss asked that I put together a spreadsheet with all of these details so that we don't lose anyone upon landing. It was totally understandable, but it felt like I needed to embark on an initial request, followed by a few days of chasing emails, until the last straggler would finally send me their flight times so that I could organize it in a spreadsheet. Just thinking about it made me tired. Instead, I had an idea. Even though Microsoft was the company-preferred supplier of internal tools, I created a Google Sheets workbook in my personal account and dropped the share link in an email to all the workshop participants. Within two hours, I had 18 individuals' accurate flight details for both the flight in and out, along with several additional comments. Each person was the "expert" on their own flight. I just created a structure in which we could interact productively. I made it possible for them to contribute in parallel, and as a result, there was much less work overall.

I felt surprised, even energized, by this experience. At the time, it was the first visible step toward the team taking ownership of their work and output. It felt like a symbolic beginning of a larger shift.

The team members were stepping out of a company leadership style that was highly centralized. They were accustomed to having someone think for them, tell them what to do, and then nag them until they did it. Instead of directing them, I ensured they had the right environment and trusted they did the right thing (because it aligned their goals with the company's). A supportive environment instills good habits that are repeated many times over and gets rid of destructive habits that undermine positive interactions.

My role was to optimize this environment to help the team achieve high productivity. In this case, my deliberate choice of a tool that allowed everyone to edit at the same time created exactly the right environment for collaboration. We could quickly get through *minutae*, and have more time for deep thought and discussion.

Structuring team interactions

Structure affects behavior and, ultimately, productivity. Ask any architect who's worked on a building with office space. If you want people to bump into one another, the shapes of the rooms influence how daily interactions happen. The environment indirectly affects group habits. Certain tasks are easier to perform, so they'll happen more often and vice versa. Any behavior, including a habit, has an implicit goal. You are better off designing or choosing the behavior you want to promote than just leaving it to the defaults of human nature.

One approach is called activity-based working. Figure out all of the activities people want to perform, prioritize them by frequency and importance, and then design a building that seamlessly supports these activities, even down to the details of the IT infrastructure. For example, when a guest comes to visit, she can just plug into the network and have seamless access to shared resources like printers.

Once people move in, seating layout and interior design add another layer. Having a team sit together physically helps them establish a rapport that helps them do their job more effectively. These can be functional teams, like the accounting department, or cross-functional teams, such as a project delivery team. At a micro level, the frequency of interaction builds better working relationships over time with the people physically close to one another.

To some extent, we lost this office context when going remote. Instead, all that's left is what we see on our screens. The software we use serves as an "architecture" for collaboration or workflow.

For example, check out the Google Sheets video by Common Craft [1] or search "google docs in plain English" on Youtube. While the examples look a bit dated, even at that point, it was clear that the added value of Google docs

---

[1] https://recommendedbyluke.com/GoogleSheetsExplainer

over other office suites was the ability to work in parallel. Word and Excel were silos. If you wanted to collaborate, you worked individually and then engaged in document ping pong.

In a digital environment, the computer screen is the two-dimensional place where work "happens". How much screen real estate do you use? How many screens are hooked up to your computer? How much time do you spend interacting with specific co-workers? How do you experience their "presence" when you are collaborating? How do you manage version control, especially when multiple people work together on the same document?

Tools and mediums structure the context of the space where online meetings happen. An interaction over email can feel very different than a quick chat message. Originally, most office software ran locally on your computer or phone. Nowadays, software is increasingly running in the browser, and it's easier to integrate and share with others.

Apologies if this sounds grandiose, but the software you use to work is your digital architecture, the digital "space" in which you work. Having been a developer in previous years, I know how much thought goes into designing features that help achieve user goals and are "functional". And most importantly, this architecture can help you or hold you back.

Screen real estate

Before digging into the details of the software your teams use, consider the hardware on which it's displayed. According to Microsoft UX Research, one of the few definitive ways to improve work-based productivity is to increase the physical screen space available:

> Significant benefits were observed in the use of a prototype, larger display, in addition to significant positive user preference and satisfaction with its use over a small display. In addition, design guidelines for enhancing user interaction across large display surfaces were identified. User productivity could be significantly enhanced in future graphical user interface designs if developed with these findings in mind. [2]

This is an option that a keen employee can afford to spend themselves, but smart managers will arrange this for everyone who wants it. It's also less of a change for employees than changing software. Alternatively, if monitors larger than the ones you already have are expensive, increase the number of screens:

> [Test subjects] edited slide shows, spreadsheets, and text documents in a simulation of office

---
[2] https://recommendedbyluke.com/MSMultiScreen

work, using each of the display arrays. Performance measures, including task time, editing time, number of edits completed, and the number of errors made, and usability measures evaluating effectiveness, comfort, learning ease, time to productivity, quickness of recovery from mistakes, ease of task tracking, ability to maintain task focus and ease of movement among sources were combined into an overall evaluation of productivity. Multi-screens scored significantly higher on every measure. [3]

Laptop docking stations, for example, are one way to increase the number of video feeds. Despite long lists of suggested gear shopping lists appearing online in March 2020, large or multiple screens were the only research-backed finding about "working from home" gear at the time.

By having multiple screens, you minimize context and task switching. People can physically move a mouse quickly across multiple screens while working on one thing. It's more in line with their actual thought processes. As a result, there is less distraction. Personally, I find it helpful to work from 3 to 4 screens because two of them always have communication channels open, e.g. Slack and MS Outlook, and then the other two are for whatever I happen to be focused on. Or it's helpful to see more of a virtual whiteboard in a workshop.

---

[3] https://recommendedbyluke.com/Multiscreen

Collaborative editing

In the context of remote and hybrid work, the most important feature of office software is the ability to edit collaboratively in real-time. [4] The software keeps track of individual changes. They are propagated to everyone else on the network and show up on their screen as soon as they arrive. Google docs was one of the earliest success stories in this space. Nowadays, many other tools that also give you the ability to edit collaboratively, like whiteboards or internal company wikis operating like Wikipedia, for example.

From a technical perspective, collaborative editing product needs to be designed and built this way from the ground up. This is a difficult nut to crack technically, due to network delays and the need to coordinate versions of work simultaneously.

The main benefit is that you don't need to have a separate step of assembling everyone's contributions into one whole. When collaborating in real-time, it's possible to use one another's contributions as further inspiration for more ideas. In an office environment geared towards collaborative editing, you shouldn't need to screen share when working together. Each person can see what's happening on their own screen, and also interact with it. This is why collaborative editing is better than having one person screen share and the rest watching.

---

[4] https://recommendedbyluke.com/CollaborativeEditingDefinition

the construction equivalent of screen sharing

The key difference is that:

1. The tool can be used by the group simultaneously.
2. They can each interact individually, and it's smart enough to prevent overwrites, for example.
3. You don't fall back on having one person using it and everyone else watching over a screen share.

If everyone can add or change what they see and hear, they can contribute without necessarily needing to hog the horn. If you allocate the time for a meeting, use tools that enable everyone to participate at once. Don't default to letting the vocal drown out the rest.

Summary

Activity-based working requires you to rethink working from home holistically, based on what you want to achieve as a company. In addition to the obvious security elements of working from home, the above-mentioned IT policy line items are the equivalent of the conference or meeting room where a meeting happens. Encouraging employees to use collaborative editing tools, and providing them a WFH allowance or buying extra monitors in the office mitigates the downside of not being physically together. It even provides additional benefits like the ability to save, copy, and work on a variation or working on a shared document in between "meetings," which wouldn't otherwise be available.

Key takeaways

- The software you use to work is your digital architecture, the digital space in which you work.
- Screen real estate affects how productive you are.
- Collaborative editing helps speed up the pace of office work.

Who needs to be involved

Ulaan Bataar, the capital of Mongolia, was physically mobile until the end of WWII. This was actually to their benefit during the war, as it was difficult to attack a city, if you didn't know exactly where it was–physically. Imagine needing to coordinate hundreds of thousands of tent owners to pack up and move 15 km west, because the greenery ensured better feed for the sheep and goats. And it was best for everyone.

This thought always makes me feel relieved when I need to implement change at a client site. In an established company, implementing changes (such as changing strategic direction) are like convincing an entire village to move, not a whole city. Everyone has their concerns, needs, and dependencies. From a social engineering standpoint, this is roughly the same level of doggedness that's required to overcome company inertia.

> "By closing the door, you create the room." –Priya Parker in *The Art of Gathering*

When preparing an effort to align across a company, the single most important question is, "who needs to be involved?"

- If you don't involve enough of the right people, you will face pushback, due to a lack of buy-in.
- If you involve too many, some participants may disconnect and disengage, feeling it's not relevant enough to their responsibilities and interests, and they become discussion deadweight for the actual participants.
- Besides representing themselves, each participant voices the concerns of groups like a department from which they hail.

Even if you don't ask all the right questions, you will generate a lot of value for everyone by ensuring that all relevant perspectives are represented. Because this often establishes working relationships among people who would otherwise never need to talk. And forcing these conversations helps create productive intra-company connections.

The meeting purpose serves as the single most important filter for deciding who needs to be included. By default, I made the mistake of trying to be too inclusive, thus unnecessarily pulling in people who didn't want to be in meetings. *When I restricted down to three or four participants, with the expectation that we would inform the rest of the company afterwards, I suddenly had a lot of eager participants hoping to be involved in a meeting.*

Decision-makers

Alignment requires the participation of decision-makers, because they make the final call. Usually, it isn't obvious what that final call should be beforehand. Even if participants might not fully agree with the approach, most will agree that a choice is necessary. And the company's decision-makers need to be involved enough in the details to be confident that everyone affected can stand behind the reasoning, even if it's inconvenient in the short term for them personally. Before you reach a conclusion, decisions often require an interpretation of how the principles driving the company can be applied to this particular situation. The purpose of exploring problems embedded in a situation is to identify how tradeoffs are being made currently, to figure out how to improve the tradeoffs in the near future.

The group's highest "ranking" person will own the decision by default and be on the hook to defend it later. Ideally, decision-makers make space for others' opinions. It's best to delay sharing a personal view until others have had the chance to speak from their own perspective. Instead, the decision-maker should be spending the first half of the meeting asking questions. This way, participants feel comfortable sharing their perspective. It's more likely they will feel heard, and you will avoid shutting down a discussion prematurely.

Later on, executive "air cover" is critical when the company needs to implement difficult decisions afterwards. The other senior figures in the company need to understand why certain decisions were made. The attending decision-maker can articulate the reasons underlying a decision to other senior people who might not have the full context, but whose teams are affected by it.

Without a sponsor behind a decision, an alignment effort may fizzle. It might be seen as a handful of corporate guerrillas who make a lot of noise, without any long-term positive change. The guerillas can't operate in a vacuum, separate from the helm of the company.

Representatives

Every major stakeholder group should have at least one representative involved. Pre-existing informal networks in your company will largely determine whether the change succeeds or not; you are best off tapping into this explicitly.

If you decide something amongst yourselves, each representative(s) will need to go back and convince their peer network of your decision, and talk through how it can be implemented in the current context.

One of the most common alignment traps is successfully aligning within one department, but then being unable to execute on that agreement due to resistance from other departments. You prevent that issue by preemptively including a representative from that department, so that he can "translate" any decisions for his co-workers. For software development teams, this can be a shared team like a "Release" team for the organization, or an "IT security" team that needs to sign off on new products before they go out to market.

Including teams you depend on will address the most common failure condition with alignment according to Harvard Business Review [5]. Alignment emerges faster on an intra-team level, as internal frictions are addressed as they come up. But it can fail to emerge across teams that have differing incentives. And executives are too far above and removed from the details to be able to address this systemic problem. So make sure the relevant voices are represented.

Doers

Also, it's important for the future viability of the whole effort to have a good mix between executives, managers, and "doers". To clarify, "doers" aren't an official title. It's just a term referring to anyone actually doing the work,

---
[5] https://recommendedbyluke.com/StrategyExecutionHBR

who has their sleeves rolled up, and who is actually in the details of making something happen. In the case of building software, this refers to the technical staff, who have a very different perspective than managers. In other contexts, it would be anyone performing the key activities of the company (which depends on what the company sells).

"Doers" are often under-represented in decision-making meetings if they aren't managers. They often have a very practical and detailed perspective that senior decision-makers lack. Their presence helps ground the discussion in practicalities, to minimize the gap between strategy and execution. Doers need to understand and buy into the new vision. After aligning, they also address doubts and answer questions among peers, which means you have buy-in at the execution level.

Other roles

1. *The brain:* usually highly intellectual and rational, able to think deeply about details on their feet, and willing to be blunt in the service of the truth. In software, these are often good techies with a high sense of responsibility for the organization.
2. *The animal spirit:* this is someone who is highly attuned to the political and organizational reality of how things happen in the company. Ideally, it's someone who knows the teams involved personally, but it can also be an external coach or advisor with lots of experience navigating organizational change.

3. *The scribe:* in some organizations, it's useful to have someone note down minutes, to have something to refer to in the future, particularly with respect to agreed responsibilities, tasks, and deadlines. Sometimes the facilitator can do this, but often it's helpful to delegate this to free up the facilitator to focus on the conversation.
4. *The timekeeper:* having someone responsible for timeboxing different phases of the discussion. When you aren't sure how much time you need to explore a topic, a timekeeper helps make sure that the meeting doesn't wander aimlessly.
5. *The taskmaster:* one person assumes responsibility for clarifying what the agreed actions are, who is picking up each one, and by when it's being done. This can be the note-taker, but sometimes it's worth splitting out this role to ensure there is enough focus on making things happen after the meeting.
6. *The cheerleader:* Keeps the meeting fun and helps motivate everyone. This is usually hard to 'recruit' for, but easy to support if you see someone already doing this occasionally.
7. *The benevolent troll:* pushes back where relevant, ideally based on facts, helps counter groupthink, and is useful during competitive games.
8. *The photographer*: takes screenshots and photos of highlights for inclusion in notes later, useful in visual workshops.
9. *The health nut:* make one person responsible for ensuring that everyone is comfortable, there are

enough breaks, and that no participant impacts another participant's physical or mental health.

All of these are optional, and it will depend on who is actually in the meeting and the number of participants. Once you decide on specific participants, think through who can serve these roles in your efforts. They can also overlap, with different participants playing multiple roles to keep the resulting discussion snappier (due to fewer participants).

Case Study: How the roles play out

For example, the company has declared innovation and cautious cash flow management as values in their public annual reports. As a company, do you value innovation more than cash flow as an organization?

A good brain would start by asking clarifying questions. If the innovation was a new color of an existing product and the cash inflow was $10 million, you would give a different answer than if the innovation was a high growth product in a new product category and the cash inflow was $1,000.

An animal spirit would be able to suggest who to talk to for more information, when to do it, and how to broach the subject. Different people will be able to help make decisions, based on their experience, and help out.

A senior decision-maker would be able to define criteria for a decision and also drive for a decision once there is enough information on the table to avoid analysis paralysis.

Having the perspectives help figure out either how to apply the strategy in a particular case, or if the strategy itself needs to be changed. If everyone at the meeting has the same role (of participant) and the same perspective, e.g. from the same department, the meeting is likely to be less productive.

Case Study: Quick buildup meetings

Sometimes the guest list at a meeting is too large. You want to decide and iterate fast. So you can split it up into a series of shorter meetings with a tighter crew. Robert Bendetti, the CFO of LifeCycle Engineering (LCE), calls this informal approach a "buildup meetings" approach.

Here's his take:

> If it's something big and strategic, and let's say there's a team of four or five working on some bigger strategic idea. You can break out into pairs of two people. And so those two call and speak. And then maybe you're adding another resource real quick.
>
> "Oh, I really think in 2023, we need to be thinking about this market."
>
> "Jessica is the leader in that market. Let's get Jessica on the horn."

So boom. You bring her up on the camera and boom, you're talking to Jessica.

"Jessica, I've been thinking about such and such. Can we do that?"

And Jessica says, "That's the dumbest idea I've ever heard. We don't do that. We tried that 10 years ago. That totally didn't work. Remember when we lost a million dollars?"

"Oh Jesus. Yes, I do. Okay. Yeah. That was really dumb. Sorry about that. Okay. Thanks."

And then boom, you're back with the two again. And then the two different groups have beat up and now you've got the big boss up there and now you're all five together. I think that can be pretty fast and more creative than if we were all in the office. I'm just not walking around everybody's office until I might call them and say:

"Hey, can we have a meeting to collaborate?"

And then they'd be like, "Yeah, I'm totally free next week. And I'll get something on your calendar for next week."

Yeah. Nobody wants to talk to the CFO, come on.

Splitting up large strategic meetings into smaller and more informal gatherings can help hash out and lay the groundwork for a larger discussion. Particularly if you are deciding strategy or making decisions about how to implement it, rapidly iterating through conversation partners can help refine proposals before a larger meeting. It also can happen immediately, rather than needing to coordinate multiple schedules.

Key takeaways

- The participant list who attends alignment meetings contributes significantly to positive outcomes, regardless of the content of the meetings.
- Consider every person above four participants very carefully, as this will slow down the discussion and decision making-especially online.
- Giving every stakeholder group a voice means they later have a stake in the solution and ultimate outcome.
- Aligning across boundaries and silos starts with having the right participants at alignment meetings.

How to contextualize when remote

When everyone moved online, they suddenly lost a lot of pre-existing context. When working with remote teams, you need to establish context deliberately and frequently. Even though you are harried, it's worth pausing to clarify context for your meeting participants or readers. Context provides meaning and clarity to your audience. Context tells the reader why you are writing, when your message is relevant, or how the new idea connects to everything else. It clarifies the purpose of your message.

Most messaging doesn't need to happen simultaneously. Important decisions, especially with many-to-many discussions required, will be made faster synchronously at a meeting. Overuse of meetings, though, has its downside too.

Trying to force meetings as the primary forum for lower priority activities, e.g. sharing project status, can burn out online meeting participants at a high enough volume. The question is what to do instead.

The Work Context Matrix

The details of how to establish context depend on how your team or company already likes to collaborate: synchronously or asynchronously. This is a really important distinction with respect to communication patterns and workflow.

To explain the difference between synchronous and asynchronous, Piotr Zagorowski of the Coffee Journeys blog uses the following analogy:

> "So I can compare it to basically being in [a] cinema, let's say, and Netflix. So if you go to the cinema, your movie is at six p.m. and it's synchronous. You just go there and everyone is there watching together. You can discuss together and go home for asynchronous work. [With asynchronous] you're just watching Netflix and you discuss it in your own time. And then you discuss with everyone who wants to

be part of the discussion, etc."

So taking the analogy to work, it's clear that there are scenarios where a synchronous approach is better, and times where asynchronous is more convenient.

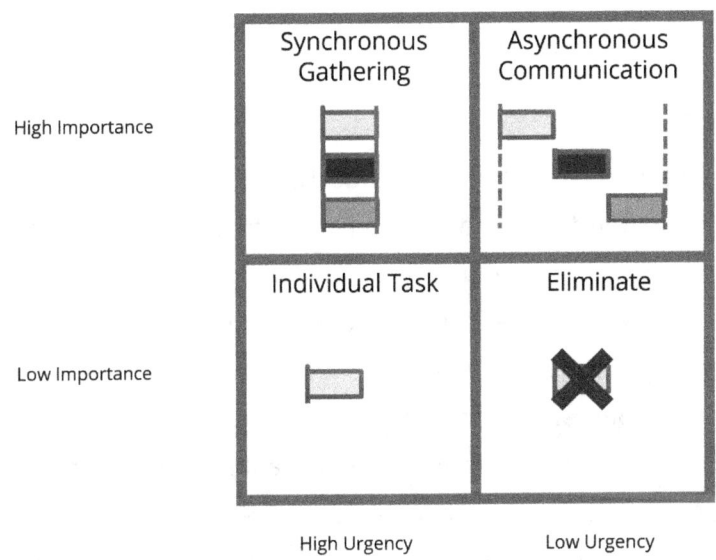

The Eisenhower/Covey priority matrix applied to remote communication patterns

In practice, if a problem or challenge is important and urgent, it should be solved synchronously. If it's important but not urgent, the asynchronous option is more convenient for the participants and can improve the overall quality of the discussion. If it's not important to the group, it can be handled outside of meetings individually or just agreed that it won't be done in order to minimize distraction and clutter.

It's also worth noting that the choice of sync vs async is quite important in the context of providing one another feedback, similar to deciding to make positive announcements publically and give constructive feedback in private 1-on-1s. How you deliver a message and when it is responded to will affect how easily it can be incorporated by the individual or team involved.

There is a potential dark side to the explosion in communication tools and methods. Every in-group has their own tool they prefer to use, so you end up needing to track many different sources at the same time. Especially if someone emails you, then tells you on MS Teams to check your email, and the follows up on your phone to discuss it. The geeks might like Slack, the business side likes Teams. In my particular case, I always follow where the key "community leads" are, because then I am certain to find them there and to be able to discuss the matter at hand. Having too many tools can be a necessary evil, and simplify as much as you can, but realize that there is a point beyond which you won't be able to go any further.

In practice, you need to be conscious of your own and your team's preferences. This is why a team contract exercise is useful. And to be deliberate when choosing how to communicate a message out to each specific person. You can even make the rules part of a team agreement. For example, billionaire Mark Cuban doesn't like meetings at all, but will default to a call if necessary. So do other busy people, like owners of big podcasts. It's up to you to define the boundaries and decision rules. Then improve them as you go.

Synchronous

Synchronous gatherings build connection and relationship more immediately, because you can see more emotion whether in-person or even on a camera. You can dig into more detail with followup questions. You can ask for or offer help immediately. It's easier to connect the dots, especially across contexts, with an in-depth synchronous discussion.

To start from the obvious, a meeting occurs at a specific time: both start and end. It's "synchronous" for all participants, where it *must* happen at the same time. This simple fact has a lot of implications.

Because most meetings are synchronous, it becomes tempting to use meetings as a "time block". Time blocks are essentially time set aside on a calendar to ensure that you do have time to work on an important task, as defined in *The One Thing* by Keller and Papasan, for example. A synchronous meeting implicitly increases the priority of a discussion, task, or decision. You are assigning people's valuable time to it. But if there are a lot of meetings, and everything feels equally high priority, then priority itself becomes meaningless. You lose a sense of relative importance, and end up feeling overwhelmed by the numbers of meetings.

Unfortunately synchronous meetings can be re-appropriated to a deadline of sorts by "calendar pirates". To increase the urgency of a task, for example preparing a status update document, you organize a meeting next week to review the document. This can be done one-to-one or with a group of stakeholders. It can even be a recurring status meeting. The meeting next week increases the urgency of a given task, but in fact, the big picture priority of the update document may still be quite low. As a result, the synchronous meeting is deadline with social pressure attached. In and of itself, the technique may make sense when used sparingly, but it loses it's value once it's used for all kinds of tasks regardless of priority.

From a synchronous meeting perspective, the more people you have in an online meeting, the more contexts you need to bring together, in order to host a useful discussion.

"Now that we're all here, let's start by pretending we work from home"

Before getting started with a meeting, you need to be setting the operational scene for the discussion. Professional office work is complicated or complex. There are many details to take into account. Having all participants up-to-date and in context helps you spend in-meeting time productively.

Establishing context is part of a larger overall trend of preparing for meetings, and not just zombie-walking into them with the hope that they will be productive.

> Cassie Solomon, the author of *Leading Successful Change*, suggests that **the antidote for having too many meetings is not even more status meetings**; it's spending more time preparing beforehand to establish context, and then following up afterwards. In particular, for every hour spent in a meeting, there should be an hour of prep and an hour of follow up for every meeting. That way, the time together has meaning because everyone attends the meeting with the right context, the right communication tools configured, and with the ability to learn and contribute their valuable perspective. From a follow-up perspective, the hour afterwards just helps to ensure that all decisions made at the meeting are being implemented. It's clear what the tasks are, who owns them, and by when they need to be done.

Meeting tips

- Jeff Bezos, Amazon's CEO, expects meeting attendees to read a 6 page memo before a meeting to set

context for the discussion.
- Alternatively, you can put on a facilitator hat: prepare an online whiteboard workspace with relevant data and input for the meeting participants, so that everyone can look at it beforehand. And then work on it together during the meeting.
- Or the participants have a reading list or a handful of pre-recorded presentations to watch beforehand, so that everyone can start discussing it during the meeting.
- Organize 'walking meetings' using a mobile phone. I personally feel more creative and focussed when I am moving physically. I really enjoyed walking meetings with stakeholders if the weather was nice before the pandemic. Nowadays, you can do what the trendy pre-teens did in the 1995 romantic comedy Clueless when cell phones were completely new: schedule a phone call with someone while you're both walking.
- Silent meetings have become popular. Organize a call where the participants don't speak. Treat it as a time-block to interact with comments on a document, for example.
- There are many variations of silent meetings which can be helpful. For example, Zapier's executive team runs their main weekly meeting this way. In the first 15 minutes, they handle the majority of open questions using Google Docs comments, and then spend the rest of the hour talking about one or two topics that need to be discussed using voice/video. Giving participants a 10-15 minute timebox at the start of a

meeting to read or review a specific document may be time well spent.

Asynchronous

To counteract the priority distortion effect, you can "meet" or communicate asynchronously. Using email, for example, or a chat tool like Slack or MS teams which is monitored in the background. Asynchronous means that each step of the communication occurs when the participants can conveniently read and respond to it. This respects everyone's time, by giving them the autonomy to decide what is important for them and to connect with others whenever it's appropriate for them. Asynchronous works well for people who benefit from long blocks of time to do creative or analytical work, what Cal Newport popularized in his book *Deep Work*.

A well-managed asynchronous strategy scales very well. There's lots of example of this among scale-ups like Hopin or Time Doctor. If you have well documented processes for example, then it's possible to hire more people to run the same process with much less coordination overhead required. All the information needed is in the documentation. One document links to any other supplemental documents, so that a full, accurate, and ideally up-to-date picture exists.

An asynchronous operating mode is very natural for teams working across many time zones. If you can resolve important queries and you aren't obsessed with getting a response *right_now*, then often the quality of the interaction goes up.

It is easier to integrate asynchronous work conversation into one's personal life. In terms of work-life integration, it's easier to both live and work according to your values when you don't have a constant stream of work deadlines and meetings to attend to. Long before the pandemic, the counterintuitive book *Total Leadership* by Stuart Friedman explored why leaders in larger companies that live according to the same values at home, at work, and in the community are not only happier but significantly more productive. Once you clarify what you want, it helps you negotiate with key stakeholders (including your kids) on all sides to truly step into an improved way to live as a professional, especially as a manager.

In practice, what often matters is the quality of thought. And not everyone thrives when put under pressure to give clever, informed, and funny answers to questions. Introverts feel less pressured socially. Particularly if there is a lot on the line.

That said, an asynchronous workflow can also slow down decision making and accountability if you aren't careful. It's very focussed on individual productivity and efficiency, which can mean that team members are very efficiently working on the wrong thing. In the book *Games at Work*, Mauricio Goldstein notes, "the lack of accountability inherent in electronic communication—the absence of an individual in the room who calls for a vote to be taken—allows decisions to be postponed indefinitely." If you are using more of an async model, it needs to be clear who is the final decision maker, what action items arise, and who on the team will be responsible for delivering them.

As much of the interaction with your remote team happens textually or visually, how you establish context when writing matters. Be painfully specific, particularly when editing your writing.

Textual

First and foremost, assume nothing. For example, some of your readers may be completely new to the topic discussed, or be company outsiders, or not really understand how your industry works.

After you draft out an email or report, re-read it asking yourself the classic journalist questions:

- Who?
- What?
- When?
- Where?
- Why?
- How?

This helps you tighten up your own thinking and identify gaps in what you are trying to say. If this extra context is included in your missive, it will help pull the reader's attention back into the right context. You are aiming to leave little unsaid.

Another really useful self-editing tip is to avoid using pronouns if possible. Instead of "she" or "he", use the person's name. Instead of they, state which department or company you are referring to.

Also avoid using 'this', 'these', 'that', or 'those'. When used in writing, demonstrative pronouns assume a shared context which may or may not actually exist.

Visual

On the visual side, context can be communicated with relative size, color, or location of items.

Use the structures that come with your online whiteboard, but also experiment with working together from a completely blank canvas. Now that people feel more comfortable with the tools, it's easier to get productive using remote visual thinking in many different domains.

Draw on your whiteboard. It's fun. Trust me. Use stick figures if you have to.

Async collaboration tips

- Document processes, so that anyone can run them. When you need to make decisions, you can just refer or link to existing documents to discuss specifics.
- Use custom templates where possible and appropriate, for speed and consistency. These can be internal or externally sourced.

- Be clear on steps but also provide context so that it's clear why and when something needs to be done.
- One approach to push your company in the asynchronous direction is to have one day a week that has no meetings. Wednesdays work well for me. If someone, especially a manager, wants to organize a meeting, they need to justify why that social contract needs to be breached to the participants.
- Automate as much of your simple workflow as you can with tools like Zapier, Make.com, Pabbly or with software. For simple tasks, this only needs to be done once and it frees up a lot of time. For more complicated interactions, design a product or service workflow with your team and automate what you can.

Key takeaways

- Synchronous meetings benefit from design up front by the organizer, pre-work for attendees, and follow up after the meeting to establish context for all collaborators
- A synchronous meeting increases the urgency of a discussion, task, or decision which needs to be done together.
- Meetings can also become a deadline of sorts.
- In order to remain effective, think and ask about your listener or reader's context, without jumping to conclusions.

- If a discussion topic is important but not urgent, consider using an asynchronous way to communicate.

How to run successful meetings

In a corporate context, it's no secret that meetings are despised as a necessary evil. For example, a vocal minority of the software developers I managed openly described them as a distraction from getting work done. There are also quite a few celebrity CEOs who openly talk down the usefulness of meetings, including Bezos, Cuban, Musk, and Dalio, all of whom have a biased perspective as CEOs and some distance from actually implementing decisions in practice. [6]

My knee-jerk reaction was to take heed of the griping and moaning. But when I started canceling loads of operational meetings (more on that later), a different contingent spoke up. They defended the need to get together or at least chat regularly on Slack. They felt the team didn't work effectively without them.

Research shows that not having enough meetings is worse than having too many. Due to conversations that don't happen, coordination suffers:

> The failure to coordinate also leads to conflicts between functions and units, and these are

---

[6] https://recommendedbyluke.com/CelebCEOMeetings

poorly handled two times out of three—resolved after a significant delay (38% of the time), resolved quickly but poorly (14%), or simply left to fester (12%).

When effective, meetings expose and then help resolve healthy conflict. These are pretty much the definition of companies with a healthy organizational culture.

Meetings are the figurative Lego blocks of company and team culture. Meetings are where directions are set, and promises are made. Any problem you experience in the culture will likely show up in the meetings held. Any gap between what is said and what happens later can often be traced back to a meeting. They're potentially the "magic moments" of high leverage in a company; but can easily turn into "mutiny moments" if what is said at the meeting differs from the day-to-day experience employees have.

There are many kinds of meetings, each brimming with their own rituals and expectations:

- Your job interview is a meeting.
- The decision to hire you happens at a meeting.
- Your onboarding happens at meetings.
- The daily ins and outs of delivery happen at meetings.
- Company strategy sessions and workshops are meetings.
- Project kickoffs and retrospectives are meetings.

- Even informal meetings like "leaving drinks" which lay the groundwork for what will happen after that person is gone.

In truth, there are many different types of meetings. Each has a different aim. The team at Lucid Meetings has an excellent list of the 16 most common ones [7]. So generalizing advice to all meetings may water down the meaning of the insight, because it matters which one you are referring to. You can look across meetings for factors relating to the subjective experience of the participants or possibly whether the outcomes were achieved.

Meetings are also where big changes happen, especially interpersonal ones within a company or across multiple external stakeholder lines. They're "where the action is", as per the title of an excellent book on meetings by Elise Keith. The goal of most meetings is to convert information into decisions. The impact achieved is affected by the quality and speed of those decisions.

> Irish author and creative coach Megan Macedo claims that the peace talks between the IRA and the British Government were successful, because they happened in a small dining room...where previously mortal enemies fell back to pleasantries, like offering to make tea for one another. It broke down stereotypes, forced them to treat each other as human beings, and laid the groundwork for a cease-fire. They stopped being strangers the moment someone got up and offered

---

[7] https://recommendedbyluke.com/MeetingTypes

> to make a cup of tea for the group. There is also something culturally embedded in the idea of eating meals and breaking bread together. People come together and become more of a community.

And the only thing worse than being forced into a meeting is not being invited to one where you think the important decisions are being made. So until someone comes up with a better alternative, meetings are here to stay.

Before getting to the remote-specific aspect, let's dig into the first principles of meetings themselves. Once you are clear on how meetings enable your company to achieve its priorities, you're ready to move meetings online effectively.

What actually matters with meetings

There are a lot of complex variables at play if we dig in to find out the truth about meetings. According to Quartz, the number of meetings held drifted up initially since the start of the pandemic, mostly increasing the number of internal meetings. Most of these were largely status meetings, based on the stats gathered by Darren Hait, author of *10x Culture*.

In contrast, nonsense meetings often try to cover up a lack of clarity, according to Thompson and Ressler in

"Why Managing Sucks". They cited a case study from GAP, the clothing retailer. Senior leader Eric Severson was surprised to see the number of meetings drop significantly (especially status meetings), once the company's expected results and outcomes were clarified. Once objectives are clear, everyone realizes these nonsensical meetings are an obstacle as opposed to a help.

To tease apart the complexity, I've found the following 3 levels to be important in both running and joining meetings in the research:

1. Whether or not the meeting achieved its aim, and whether the aim was well-defined and truly in line with what's best for the company as a whole in the first place.
2. How participants feel about the meeting, as that drives what happens after the meeting and includes the social interaction among them, especially for people who don't know each other.
3. The meeting's mechanics, logistics and practicalities

The primary aim of a meeting ideally comes out of a well-defined context and priorities that have already been established. And if not, then alignment is your top priority. Because all of your other meetings are proportionately going to be less fruitful and worthwhile. If you only optimize for the feel-good factor, you'll be coddling your participants but not achieving anything. If you only look at mechanics, you'll avoid the obvious errors made by meeting organizers and leaders, but not necessarily getting to where you need to as a company.

Once you get the basics in place, though, you need to realize that great meetings happen because of the interpersonal dynamics. In *Art of Gathering*, Priya Parker states, "we inadvertently shrink a human challenge down to a logistical one. We reduce the question of what to do with people to a question of what to do about things: PowerPoint presentations, invitations, AV equipment, cutlery, refreshments." These are universal basics that need to be in place to remove friction for the participants, but in and of themselves, these basics don't help define or achieve a group outcome.

Ideally, you think through an intended outcome beforehand and then structure the meeting to achieve it. This is what I mean by designing a meeting. If you set up the boundaries correctly, you can pull in and enable all the meeting participants to contribute. And to walk away from the meeting with buy-in to the outcome.

Finally, you have the impact of the actual logistics. You can read about them in advice to budding meeting organizers (including remote meeting organizers at the start of the pandemic). The research clarifies that some of this matters to attendees and the company, and some of it only looks good.

1. Meeting purpose

One of the fastest ways to figure out if you need a meeting is to clarify the intended outcome for the meeting or a meeting series. By outcome, I'm referring to a metric you are hoping to improve, as well as a target value. Once you achieve that target value, the meeting has outlived its usefulness. This meeting design heuristic from *The Surprising Science of Meetings* by Steven Rogelberg cuts through lots of red tape. If you don't have a clearly defined desired outcome, then propose one first. Otherwise, the meetings will feel like a heavy-handed process that gets in the way, rather than an enabler of outcomes.

There are many alternative ways to monitor status. Using meetings for this is like trying to crack an egg with a baseball bat instead of a teaspoon. Yes, it can work in the short term, but it's arguably an inadvertent abuse of power that can cause more problems than it solves.

Ask each participant how they want to keep you up-to-date, and at what cadence. You can also discuss how they'll handle exceptional situations while you are at it. If you let them own status updates, it will be in their interest to have something good to report honestly. Having informal demos of "what's new" on a regular basis should be enough to trigger useful discussions, without the need to prepare status presentations.

When the team doesn't progress, you can use meetings to figure out why. In short, there may be no need to hold a weekly status meeting "proactively" for every single project or product.

The term *status-itis* conveys this unhealthy over-focus on status. It can communicate a lack of trust, low expectations, and an unwillingness to delegate ownership to the team that needs it most:

- The ones actually doing the work.
- Having the most relevant context.
- Often being asked to make decisions quickly.

The cost of such *status-itis* can be significant. Taking 30 minutes of the participants' time every week does ensure you get updates synchronously and by a certain time. Yet, this is time they don't spend being productive. Instead of working, they also need a few hours or days to prepare their message for the meeting. As an alternative, you can request a written report on a cadence. Yes it implies you will need to read it. Ultimately, anyone who is interested can stay in the know at their leisure. Meet, if necessary and not by default. Or better yet, design a dashboard that keeps an accurate status in real-time, like an operational heartbeat tracker, so that you don't need either.

Instead of monitoring status in fear of something going wrong, clarify and motivate how each person can contribute to clear company outcomes using 1-on-1 meetings. Each person already has their own drives, interests, passions, skills, abilities, and responsibilities. In order to take advantage of this, alignment is where you start. Uncover inherent motivations. Explore how they would fit into an overall purpose.

While I didn't do this on a cadence because I had too many immediate direct reports to make it possible, even doing it pragmatically when needed will provide a lot of insight. Especially when getting started with a new team, it's worth using this technique. It help you figure out the "lay of the land", according to Michael Watkins in his classic handbook for new leaders, *First Ninety Days*. Afterwards, the working relationships you establish help create a safe space to raise difficult or sensitive topics.

One-on-ones are extremely powerful, because they are personal and build up the manager-employee relationship. The book *12*, by Wagner and Harter from the Gallup Organization, discusses a factory floor manager who systematically used one-to-ones to generate ideas for improvement, which she then acted on. This, in turn, built up a lot of trust:

> "To discover how to better manage her team, Górska-Kołodziejczyk began having individual meetings with the workers. 'I started with listening to them, what they have to say, how they see it, how they want the work to be organized, what more they expect, what kind of work materials are they lacking,'' she said. 'At the same time, I wrote down the problems and issues they wanted to be resolved. When we met again, I gave a report on what had been done. It also brought us closer.' She disregarded comments that she was mothering her employees and followed her instincts."

In addition to building trust into the relationship, this approach helps identify the concerns of all decision-makers preemptively, e.g., when a new idea is raised in a large meeting. In some cases, it helps to clear the decks of the easy fixes, so that you can have larger meetings for bigger problems.

I also had that experience when I initially needed to troubleshoot the group disengagement on technical design calls. Most of the meeting participants were tuned out. I couldn't see them, as everyone had video feeds disabled. I suspect they were just muted and doing other things, some productive, some not. For the majority, the meeting experience was like hearing background music, while doing something else. When I spoke with the team members individually to reconnect, it was clear they were keen on the work. The group dynamic needed to be fixed. After completing multiple 1-to-1s, I felt it was easier to discuss the tasks at hand in a more relevant way to them individually, even when we were meeting as a group. The same pattern worked with stakeholders and in other contexts.

2. The emotional and social meeting context

Buying decisions are typically made using emotions and then justified rationally; in the same way, meeting "next steps" require enough emotional power to ensure that participants follow through on them, regardless of the decision's rationale.

Think about it. An individual half-heartedly agrees with what was discussed at a meeting. His opinion wasn't asked for. He doesn't feel socially connected with the other participants. Why would he care to follow through and take action? I'd be more surprised if he followed through, rather than if he didn't. If that is the scenario, the meeting is likely to be unsuccessful in inviting that participant to contribute and "own" whatever was agreed.

Admittedly, some outliers do have an oversized sense of obligation and duty. But most don't.

There are two parts to this:

1. The individual's emotional experience during the meeting. Do they feel involved or bored? Are they frustrated? Angry? Adventurous? Exhilarated?
2. The social context of the meeting and the relationships the participants have, both in the company hierarchy and their informal connections within the company (who they do beers or teas with).

This emotional context serves as a subconscious pre-filter for any content in a meeting, for any decision they ultimately make. Do the participants naturally:

- Engage and drive toward a topic
- Disengage, avoid, or fight a topic

If any meeting participant is disengaged, avoidant, or combative, they don't get value from that part of the meeting. For example, if participants "fight over nothing", it's about a participant's autonomous emotional state. A fight response was triggered for one of the participants.

This comes from the classic model of the "triune brain". The neocortex handles rational and analytical work, and is uniquely human. The emotional inner part of the brain is shared with all mammals and relates to our emotional lives. And the very core of our brains, which we share with reptiles, like the basal ganglia, drives a lot of the autonomous behavior of our bodies.

And more importantly, the lizard brain drives a freeze, fight, or flight response that helped prehistoric lizards outrun predators. We inherited this wetware and the associated response from our lizard ancestors. Now, it affects our day-to-day zoom calls. It influences what we notice. It influences when we lock up and disengage. And it is tied to our underlying focus and motivation, what we want to go after.

This lizard brain serves as a "pre-filter". Brain research has confirmed that the lizard brain reaction is faster than the mammalian brain, which in turn is faster than the human brain. During a meeting, participants will respond first using the lizard brain to anything that comes up. If that is a negative response, it will prevent the other two parts of the brain from engaging with other participants.

It's difficult to consciously calm down the lizard brain, especially for the person being overstimulated, because they "can't read the label while they are in the bottle." If the participants' lizard brains are overstimulated, especially if the fight-flight-freeze mechanism is engaged, then often they will disrupt or sabotage the meeting goal, usually subtly. The "disengage" response is a flight mechanism. The content doesn't resonate emotionally with that person. And it's very hard to address that in a larger group, thus the importance of keeping meetings as small as possible. The larger a group is, the more likely that kind of reaction happens.

This invisible lizard brain "force field" explains the subtext of what happens at meetings. It's admittedly a strange concept, but I've found it quite useful to explain why a meeting goes off the rails. In spite of feeling socially connected and rationally engaged with a group, it only takes one hyperactive lizard brain to derail a meeting. Once I saw and understood this dynamic, I couldn't "unsee" it.

In my opinion, these pre-emotional factors are why meetings are often disliked, despite the fact that they underlie how the organization actually works as a "herd" of people's lizard brains.

They strongly influence factors like attention and focus, for example. In the classic software management book *Peopleware*, Tom DeMarco notes: "Imperfect attention at meetings is more about a dysfunctional meeting culture than about anyone's work ethic." That dysfunctionality occurs at this pre-emotional level. Do participants feel safe? Can they speak their minds without fear of counter-attack or reprisal? Will their opinions be taken into account? Is hiding a better strategy?

Implicitly, this reaction connects to an atavistic fear of being excluded from the group. Does their voice matter to the organization?

It's hard to separate out the emotional undertones from the social aspect of meetings. In *The Art of Gathering*, author Priya Parker quips, "Gatherings that are willing to be alienating—which is different from being alienating—have a better chance to dazzle." This isn't about actually stonewalling or excluding people. It's the fear of being excluded, which isn't the same thing. Personally, I was afraid of speaking up for years when I was a front-line employee. When I finally worked up the courage to raise issues, I did so with mixed success. But at least I was raising them. And sometimes, it helped. Other times, it fell on deaf ears. It was the fear of speaking up that held me back.

Another important way this factor shows up is a fear of change and uncertainty. Humans prefer to make wrong decisions rather than to hover in a state of uncertainty. Be prepared for resistance to anything new. I personally struggled with this. For this reason, I avoided raising issues that were affecting me, in some cases, for years. Resistance to change is natural. Raising objections is a prerequisite to changing decisions and getting aligned around a new approach.

The best way to start meetings, especially ones you expect will include difficult conversations, is by sharing specific details you have observed. In *The Art of Gathering*, Priya Parker notes that, "specificity is a crucial ingredient. The more focused and particular a gathering is, the more narrowly it frames itself and the more passion it arouses." Abstract concepts are a barrier to understanding. They also tend to flatline the emotional undertone, as meeting participants spend a lot of mental bandwidth trying to understand the concepts.

In contrast, it helps to discuss specific details when tackling a particular problem or story. People naturally think in terms of stories. It's much easier for participants to generalize and problem-solve using the particulars of a situation than to apply a theoretical framework they picked up somewhere.

In addition to what the meeting is about, this emotional layer helps understand and explain what happens during and after the meeting even more. This emotional drive affects decisions made during the meeting and how they are implemented afterward. If I can just promise things in meetings, even though I don't connect with the decisions emotionally, I won't do them. If there are other accountability mechanisms in place, ones that motivate me over and above what is said in larger meetings, then maybe I will.

One of the more powerful accountability mechanisms is team dynamics. Once you have a true team relying on one another to deliver an end product, you will see them supporting each other while holding themselves accountable.

The best way to address this layer is to structure your meetings for participation and collaboration, especially if run online. By this, I mean paying attention to how much input each participant provided during the meeting, i.e. time spent speaking vs. overall time spent. Bart Doorenwert, the author of the *Peer Learning Guide*, puts it well:

"What interaction really means, what people

are looking for is more control over interacting and contributing in a group setting, especially when you're looking at a remote situation. I think one of the hardest things I had to figure out online is how to give people control over what topics they want to raise, if they want to dive deeper into something. How do you halt the process and focus on that? How do you give people a sort of a menu or things to choose from so they can pick where they want to talk about rather than me determining? We're going to talk about this."

In short, this means heavily limiting time spent in one-to-many communication patterns like presentations in favor of formats like #LeanCoffee[8], Gamestorming[9], or Agile games like retrospectives. This forces people to interact and learn from one another, which engages them and helps them work better together. The next chapter will focus more on how to move existing meetings online, focusing on this area in particular.

Another way of looking at improving this layer of meetings comes from the blog of Daniel Coyle, the author of *The Culture Code*: [10]

1. Talk less
2. Help others talk more

---

[8] https://leancoffee.org
[9] https://www.gamestorming.com
[10] https://recommendedbyluke.com/MeetingCheatSheet

3. Call on the person with the least status first, to diffuse status management (which is highly a counterproductive group dynamic)

3. The mechanics and logistics of meetings

Finally, it makes sense to address the structure and logistics around meetings and how they affect meeting effectiveness. Surprisingly, this has been studied rigorously, and there are useful takeaways here over and above the commonly received wisdom. There was a flurry of articles and content around this topic at the start of the pandemic. Well-meaning, but just the outer layer of what matters, compared to the other two factors. The two key concepts are perceived meeting quality (PMQ) and net positive impact (NPI).

PMQ digs into the subjective experience of meeting participants. A study from 2011 [11] on 367 participants of 18 meeting design characteristics details the statistically significant takeaways of actions that consistently increase any meeting's perceived quality:

- Being deliberate about the purpose and meeting participants, as discussed earlier
- An agenda prepared and proposed <u>before</u> the meeting

---

[11] https://recommendedbyluke.com/MeetingsStudy

- Starting on time and finishing on or before time, even if all attendees haven't arrived yet
- Arranging an appropriate space and/or tooling needed to achieve the meeting's purpose, including temperature and lighting
- Providing snacks and beverages, in a way that doesn't distract from the purpose
- Agreeing "topical and behavioral" ground rules for the meeting, even informally. Ground rules need to be discussed and established and posted for everyone to see.

For anyone who has organized meetings, these are all frequently brought up as ideas for improvement by individuals after a get-together. It seems they are more sources of cognitive load and friction, which distract the participants from the purpose of the meeting. In other words, they are necessary but not sufficient to have happy meeting participants consistently. It forms a decent baseline of what needs to be in place for effective participation.

In contrast, NPI focuses on the Net Positive Impact a meeting has, measuring how the meeting resulted in something positive. Sometimes, the declared objectives and outcomes aren't reached, but there can be a positive outcome. It's explored, refined, and applied in detail in Elise Keith's wonderful book *Where the Action Is*.

Elise defines effective meetings this way:

> In the case of meetings, the "natural resources" they deplete can include time, energy, intellec-

tual stimulation, emotional satisfaction, money, and forward momentum (to name a few!). Effective meetings create more of these resources than they use up.

While you do want to produce decisions and next steps from meetings, NPI gives you a sense of how much meetings are contributing to or taking away from your workplace. First and foremost, the most observable impact will be on the meeting's participants. If they are keen to have another one, because they find the meetings fulfilling, that speaks for itself. Of course, the impact could be much wider than the team, or even the company, with a broader social impact.

As a team productivity tool, meetings are a double-edged sword. They can be used to drive completion by imposing a deadline, at which results need to be presented. They can be run as a workshop, to do the work together during the meeting, rather than only meeting to discuss status. Or they can be eliminated to provide as much "white space" to minimize distraction for individual team members.

Even more important than individual meetings is getting the right sequence of meetings in place. A meeting workflow enables teams to achieve high performance. Designing for psychological flow, as coined by Mihaly Csikszentmihalyi in his book called *Flow*, is the key consideration here. As Elise Keith says, "too many meetings block the flow. So do too few."

Despite potentially seeming a bit annoying, scheduling is an important logistical factor for highly distributed teams. Coordination of calendars, particularly among high level stakeholders and team members distributed across multiple time zones, significantly affects when meetings are possible. This, in turn, can affect the frequency and quality of the meetings. It takes longer to achieve that impact, if you have to wait two weeks for all of the executives to be available at the same time across 13 time zones, just to make a decision. Ultimately, this impacts productivity. To some extent, this effect can be mitigated with meetings on a cadence. You can discuss less urgent topics at the next pre-arranged get-together which happens every 2 Tuesdays. But you risk creating too many crypto-status meetings if you aren't careful.

Finally, the main intention behind meetings is often to identify and agree next action steps, in the context of the overall intended outcome. Any meeting which doesn't result in that is quite possibly a waste of time. Wolf's Law of Meetings states, "The only important result of a meeting is agreement about next steps." This underlines the importance of closing the meeting with a summary of:

- Next steps
- Clear ownership for individual steps
- Any agreed dates or time frames

Being clear on why a time frame exists is helpful. Particularly, it would be good for all participants to understand business consequences of hitting or missing different dates. This way, you respect everyone's time while ensuring that business needs are served.

Documenting the agreed next steps, helps prevent people from forgetting what was agreed or misinterpreting it. Ideally, this happens during a visual exploration on a whiteboard. Having a living document of what happened at the meeting helps hold the participants accountable to one another. At minimum, a follow up email from the note taker suffices.

Key takeaways

- Being mindful and deliberate about the purpose of each meeting will help you focus during the meetings you have, and cancel the ones which aren't moving the ball forward for you.
- Work on specifics, by framing problems as stories during meetings, to engage all meeting participants and motivate them with the topic at hand.
- Coordination of calendars, particularly with high-level stakeholders and teams distributed across multiple time zones, significantly affects the speed at which alignment is possible.
- When discussing next steps, make it clear what needs to be done, by whom, by when, and what the business implications are of the agreed dates.

How to move meetings online successfully

In my free time, I organized meetups around innovation topics in London. And one of the most popular small-event formats we used was something called #LeanCoffee[12]. A random group of ideally 12 people showed up over a coffee and a breakfast muffin. Everyone wrote down potential discussion topics or questions on post-its, described or pitched them, and then we voted. Based on this democratic process, we figured out the most popular topics of the day. We then used that to construct an agenda for the remainder of the gathering. We used a timer for each step to give enough time for each step, and check whether everyone was still interested in the topic after the timebox was hit.

The beauty of this approach was that:

- Popular topics were covered.
- Individual topics were raised and pitched, so if they weren't covered by the group, individuals could discuss them privately afterward.
- We didn't need to prepare, as long as we facilitated effectively.

---

[12] https://www.leancoffee.org

Lean Coffee is one of several workshop formats called a "real-time agenda", where you discover the main topics of the day and then discuss the most important ones until they run out.

After running these every two weeks for a few years, I started using them as a meeting format with a corporate client. In particular, any exploratory discussions like retrospectives helped all participants raise and explore the key concerns without having the meeting overrun. Interestingly enough, I managed to start doing this with distributed teams using online tools. Initially, I found a free tool called ideaboardz.com[13], which had the basic features and didn't require me to get budget.

As the teams became increasingly comfortable with this approach, it was easy to adapt online whiteboard tools like miro.com[14] or mural.co[15] for a similar structure. It was like an un-workshop workshop. Once everyone was familiar with the tools and approach, it also didn't require much prep work. Still, it helped surface any major issues the team was facing. The discussion gleaned a list of specific action items (often for me) to be taken. Often these were related to a problem area, a risk, or a bottleneck. By the next time we ran another one of these meetings a few weeks later, I'd usually managed to address most of those action steps.

---

[13] https://ideaboardz.com
[14] https://www.miro.com
[15] https://mural.co

What made this online transition of the #LeanCoffee format successful

A great online meeting is a structured collaboration, where nearly all participants contribute and listen to what others are providing. Originally, I'd discovered this principle in the context of peer-to-peer learning, as per Bart Doorenwert's *Peer Learning Guide*[16] and Dave Gray's *Gamestorming*[17], particularly for in-person workshops. Fortunately, since I discovered this approach, the technology has now matured enough that this is possible to do (although you do need to experiment to find a combination that works for your teams). It helped that I already had some in-person facilitation experience from running meetups, but everyone has to start somewhere.

The most important aspect of this is to create or adapt a meeting structure to your team's objectives, while giving them the space to provide the content. To lead with what is currently on their mind. There are 16 meeting types in the Lucid Meeting hierarchy of most common meetings, so it's in your interest to build this collaborative element into them as much as possible. It can mean using whiteboards. It can work with tools like Google Docs, which allows everyone to edit and contribute in real-time. But most importantly, it requires you to let go of centralized control, and trust that the group will provide something better than you could hone, refine, and own

---
[16] https://www.peerlearning.is
[17] https://www.gamestorming.com

individually as a group leader.

The best framework for collaboration online comes from Alex Pentland, the head of MIT's Connection Science and Human Dynamics lab. Overall, Pentland's studies show that team performance in meetings is driven by five measurable factors:

1. Everyone in the group talks and listens in roughly equal measure, keeping contributions short.
2. Members maintain high levels of eye contact, and their conversation and gestures are energetic.
3. Members communicate directly with one another, not just with the team leader.
4. Members carry on back-channel or side conversations within the team.
5. Members periodically break, go exploring outside the team, and bring information back to share with others.

Using these factors alone, [18] Pentland has been able to predict correctly which teams will win a business plan contest, the financial results that teams making investments would achieve, when team members will report that they've had a "productive" or "creative" day. Note that everything except for eye contact and gestures can be done online without video-based meeting tools. Instead of eye contact, there are other indicators of intent from discussion participants in software that you use. You need to pay attention to those behavioral cues in meetings.

---

[18] https://recommendedbyluke.com/pentlandHBR

Most importantly, though, the meeting lead or facilitator drives or dis-incentivizes all of the above, based on the meeting's structure or design. If you design a small group meeting as a webinar with one person speaking for an hour, the meeting is pointless. And meeting design lies well within a meeting organizer's control, even when remote.

Pentland's approach explains why the LeanCoffee structure engages people, and what to look for when designing or selecting your own meeting structures. Make it possible for meeting participants to participate fully-with everyone else attending-and keep it lively.

Working visually

Another major reason why LeanCoffee worked both offline and online was the visual component of the discussion. Other than building in collaboration, having a visual component help to keep a discussion less abstract. When you have one idea per post-it, for example, there is a specific place that the post-it exists relative to all other ideas. Physical or virtual post-its can be used as placeholders to keep track of complexity, interrelationships, and priorities among multiple ideas.

Working visually is critical in a remote context. Not only is "a picture worth a thousand words", but also visual indicators in the software you use to communicates other people's intent. They serve the same function as body language cues. It helps to know who has a document open or where each person's cursor is. If working visually works for a random group of strangers, like at an in-person Lean Coffee event, it should be possible to make it work within one company among colleagues.

Post-its and icons

It's worth noting that post-its here are powerful as place-holders for a concept; a post-it serves as a symbol for anything you want it to in the context of a conversation. I first came across this when discovering agile ways of working. In the context of a kanban board, a card is not meant to fully specify what needs to be done. It is a short description, left as a placeholder for a conversation on that topic. If the discussion warrants it, one post-it can be broken into multiple other post-its. It can also serve as a symbol for anything else, like a component of a system, a conversation topic, a team member, etc.

At their core, post-its themselves aren't valuable, even if you have a lot of them. They are just an artifact of a useful conversation. They enable groups to hold conversations in line with Pentland's 5 factors, even when online. Exploring the interrelationships among the concepts is what's valuable, especially when this is done with all stakeholders. That's why they are valuable.

Colors

Over time, a team evolves meaning within the tools you use. For example, look at Shishir Mehrotra's use of color on whiteboards [19] to support a decision-making process. Shishir is the founder and CEO of Coda. Colors helped clarify their thought process, although he freely admits that consistency matters more than the individual colors they use. [20] The same colors mean the same things. Here's their approach:

- Black: question
- Blue: option
- Gray/brown: example
- Purple: highlight
- Green/red: pro/con
- Orange: conclusion

Color helps clarify the stage they are at with any given decision. But most importantly, this color coding helps them explore many alternatives, and identify key underlying questions. They call these eigenquestions [21], i.e. questions where, if answered, likely answers tens of subsequent questions as well. Great framing starts by searching for the most discriminating question of a set — the eigenquestion. [22]

Drawing

Drawing, even cartooning with stick figures if necessary, puts yet another spin on the topic(s) at hand. As

---

[19] https://recommendedbyluke.com/CodaColor
[20] https://recommendedbyluke.com/CodaConsistency
[21] https://recommendedbyluke.com/Eigenquestions
[22] https://recommendedbyluke.com/FramingEigenquestions

Gamestorming CEO Dave Mastronardi points out, any actual drawing during a workshop is not only fun, it helps participants exit their comfort zone and also tap into other parts of their brains. In an online setting, this could mean uploading photos of hand-drawn sketches or piggybacking on icons or images found online.

All of these techniques can be applied to the meeting itself. When online, it's much easier to copy-paste and explore different variants and prototypes of an agenda or meeting template. You can iterate fast. If your notes are taken visually as the discussion enfolds, it's easy to rearrange or regroup individual pieces to make more informed and accurate decisions with information from all participants.

In short, if you are organizing meetings online, try to hook into as many of these visual collaboration features as you can during your meeting. It will maximize engagement and the perceived quality of the meeting. Your attendees will achieve the meeting objectives.

Not every meeting needs to be run in a Lean Coffee style or as a workshop, but operational meetings must ensure that everyone can participate and raise what they think is most pressing, so that the group gets the most out of the meetings. And most importantly, the basics of meetings still apply. For example, close meetings with specific next steps and deadlines for specific attendees.

Key takeaways

- Choose a structure that helps the group achieve its

objectives.
- Go visual in parallel with the conversation.
- Clarify who owns what at the end of the meeting and follow up afterward.

Top 15 tips when running your meetings online

1. There may be conflict, but then it's your role to help the group navigate through the uncertainty. Priya Parker, author of *The Art of Gathering*, says, "part of the role of a host is to practice generous authority. And I define generous authority as doing three things with your guest. [The first] is to connect them to each other and to the purpose. To protect them from each other. And to temporarily equalize them." You need to ensure that everyone feels safe enough to say what they truly mean. Avoiding conflict leads to abdication of responsibility. Too much conflict over minor points will be an unproductive distraction. Participants will have different perspectives and experiences to contribute, especially if a cross-functional team is meeting. The end goal is to help the group make meaningful decisions and achieve the meeting's purpose.
2. From a practical perspective, particularly in a distributed team, you need to find meeting times that work for everyone. This can mean spanning full executive calendars, and either convincing them to meet

now or finding a future time that works for everyone. It also needs to take into account time zones. When you have teams across multiple time zones, it will usually mean that you have limited overlap across calendars. In my case, it usually meant that remote all-hands meetings could only be scheduled from 11am-3pm my time (and even that required certain team members to be up at 5am for part of the year).
3. Admittedly, many of the perceived meeting quality (PMQ) recommendations from the research are focused on offline meetings. In order to adapt this to online meetings, it's probably fair to say that:
    - Online meetings need even more preparation, planning and thought about content, participants, and structured interactions than in-person meetings.
    - The software tools being used to facilitate the meeting create a digital space where people interact.
    - Do you have enough breaks or structured interactions, so that participants can address physiological needs like food, drink, and non-work commitments (for a longer meeting like a workshop)? In particular, think through the context for the interaction, especially for a larger group. Do your tools allow participants to edit content in real-time and participate collaboratively? How will you handle breakouts of a larger group into smaller working groups? How can participants choose to self-organize or indicate interest in a particular topic to shift the direction of

the conversation?

4. Be deliberate about who needs to be invited to every meeting. This is especially true for cross-functional or strategic teams. In online meetings, the bar seems very low. It's easy to keep adding people because there aren't any physical constraints. So only add people who you know will spend most of the meeting both contributing and listening. They need to "earn" their right to participate, because your goal should be to maximize participation. Nominate one person responsible for each of the roles previously mentioned, e.g. taking and distributing notes to absent invitees. Ideally, offload work from the facilitator or meeting lead, so that they can be focused on the big picture discussion.

5. Prepare topics for the meeting and distribute them. This can be a formal agenda. It can be a couple of post-its. Ideally, you can poll the group for topics. For example, I've successfully shared a link to an empty whiteboard and asked participants to contribute topics for a biweekly retrospective as they come up. At the end of every two weeks, we logged onto that whiteboard, and had several topics to prioritize and discuss. We spent less time in the meeting coming up with ideas, and as a result, we enjoyed more time to discuss these topics.

6. Once you get into the details of any given meeting, figure out what meeting interaction "rules" work for you and your team, similar to Amazon CEO Jeff Bezos's six-page writeup or Shark Tanker Mark Cuban only taking calls if necessary or in-person meetings

to get a check:
- What are the tradeoffs and preferences in play?
- What are you optimizing for? (see company and team goals)
- What does your team care about? These are likely to differ significantly based on meeting type, so it's best to think through each meeting individually. This is most useful for any recurring meetings, since the total time spent in them is much larger.

7. After assembling everyone, open each meeting with a clear statement of purpose. Read it from the agenda if you have to. As obvious as this is, I had an annoying habit of inviting a group of people to a problem-solving meeting, and assuming that having them all on a call was enough to start talking about it. When they finally pushed back, I realized that my role as a facilitator was to establish context by describing the problem and detailing all known consequences of the problem. This helped everyone establish how much heat was coming from the "burning platform," and often directed the group to a better outcome because they knew what was at stake.

8. Make sure that everyone understands and agrees this purpose. In particular, you may be using unnecessarily vague language. Be open to honing that statement of purpose. Although it might feel counterproductive, establishing the right direction and aligning around it is the best possible way to spend your time, until you are aligned. You may discover you need to reconvene for a larger meeting, if there

is significant disagreement at this stage. Once you have agreed on a meeting purpose, get into the thick of it.

9. If you can, limit one-way presentations in remote meetings to ten minutes. Imagine it's a talking-head video on YouTube. You only watch it because you have to. If you think about presentations from the participants' subjective experience, you'll see that one-way broadcasts are quickly forgotten unless they are extremely highly designed and produced. Most participants clock out after ten minutes anyway. You have everyone's full attention for the first two minutes, and it goes downhill from there. And most people will also remember the end of a presentation. If you must deliver more content, make a series of short videos and have people watch them on their own time in preparation for the meeting. The meeting time can then be used to discuss viewed content.

10. Design for in-meeting interaction, as much as possible:
    - Ask the silent person their opinion.
    - Start a debate.
    - Argue against your own points to show that you are keen on making the best possible decision, even if it means your initial angle was wrong.

11. Note that brainstorming and prioritizing use different parts of the human brain. One of the classic pieces of advice for kids learning how to write in grade school is to avoid editing, when drafting your text. The same carries over to meetings. In

Gamestorming[23] terms, these are called divergent and convergent thinking. Divergent is about right-brain creativity, while convergent refers to left-brain analysis. In between, you can playfully explore the options you came up with, depending on how much time you have. Based on this insight, divide up the agenda into the divergent, exploratory, and convergent parts of the meeting. At the beginning of the meeting, after framing the purpose or problem, talk about all of your options and brainstorm more as a group if that's helpful. Explore those options. And then converge on one solution, decision, or come up with a bunch of action steps to help validate the discussed options.

12. During online meetings, it's beneficial to have everyone looking at the same thing with the possibility of contributing. This visual component engages everyone. It's also helpful to solicit input that doesn't require talking. People can help add ideas to a Google Sheets workbook while others talk. This not only makes the meeting happen in more senses (literally), the information is richer, and also it becomes much easier to work in parallel across all participants...not just one talking head at a time.

13. Use this visual context to structure your interactions. Online whiteboard tools or kanban boards often include different templates which can be used as a jumping-off point for your discussions. You can give additional meaning to a group of ideas by putting

---

[23] https://www.gamestorming.com

them in a box. Or pre-emptively putting a few boxes up to prompt more specific types of responses. For example, as part of a retrospective, you can add boxes for suggestions about what to start doing, what to stop doing, and what to continue doing. This visual container makes it safe to raise difficult topics, like what to stop doing. This could apply to either one individual or a team.

14. Thinking out loud visually with post-its also means that it's easier to handle the cognitive load of complicated topics with lots of moving parts:
    - There is a record of the group's thought process after the meeting.
    - If there are longer-running concerns, participants can meet again to pick up where they left off.
    - Even subgroups of the meeting participants can convene to drill down on particular parts of the overall picture to refine the thinking in a specific area.

15. Speaking of wrapping up, make sure you leave enough time to wrap up and summarize the actionable takeaways. Who will do what, and by when? The more expensive the team members involved in a meeting, the more important (and valuable) this step is. If no one follows through, the time spent during the meeting is 100% wasted. As the organizer or facilitator, be prepared to spend at least as much time following up on agreed action steps as long as the meeting itself took. This can include individual conversations,

follow-up meetings as a group or an asynchronous format.

Key takeaways

- More preparation and thought up-front helps meetings be more productive.
- Consider what you do before, during, and after a meeting, and whether you can improve any of those 3 areas.

What you can do now

The following approach helps you evaluate how your teams spend time. Figure out where you need meetings and where you're currently wasting time. You can audit your personal meetings on your own by gathering your personal meeting data. Even if it's subjective, you can figure out what meetings you can cancel or restructure. If you get pushback from others, you can justify your suggested changes by sharing this analysis.

Meeting quality audit

Start with your own calendar. You have the most relative control over your agenda:

1. Audit your meetings last month. Just get an overview of any patterns or trends in your meetings.
2. Figure out what types of meetings they are. Categorize them. You can use colors in Outlook or Google calendar to see the categories visually. In particular, note down what percent of your time you spend in status meetings. As a rule of thumb, this shouldn't exceed 25%, according to Andy Grove, the former CEO of Intel and author Peter Drucker. You need "white space" to think deeply about and respond to current challenges.

3. Export a typical week or two of meeting names. Look for the latest on exactly how to do this:
   - Google Calendar [24]
   - MS Outlook [25]
   - Also, consider exporting an .ics file from Google calendar and importing it into MS Outlook. Export from Outlook, as it has better support for spreadsheet-friendly formats like comma-separated values (CSV).
4. Add a column. For each meeting, define a purpose, and type out why this meeting exists.
5. Add a column where you calculate how much time is scheduled per meeting. Sum up time spent by category. The data you've collected serves as a baseline for further investigation.
6. Once you have defined the meeting purposes, grade each meeting type with a subjective quality score (0-100%). This grade should reflect how well you think each meeting type achieves its objectives. Alternatively, you can break out:

- How you feel about a meeting, and
- How well it achieves its purpose

The above can be articulated as two separate grades. Then multiply them together to get one number per meeting. Take the square root to smooth out the extremes numerically. Finally, sort all meetings based on this score

---

[24] https://recommendedbyluke.com/GCalExport
[25] https://recommendedbyluke.com/MSOutlookExport

from the lowest to highest. Consider frequency when you get an ordered list, starting with your lowest quality meetings.

Experiment with an existing meeting

From the above, choose a specific recurring meeting that is important to you and where the quality is low (< 80% in your subjective opinion.) Ideally, choose one of the top meetings in the previously generated list.

First of all, consider if you can cancel it completely. You may discover recurring meetings you can cancel if they don't fulfill their purpose or if the purpose is no longer important. Freeing up people's calendars will be a welcome surprise. If you ever need to bring the meetings back, it's easy to revert your decision.

If not, try to talk the participants into reducing the cadence. In other words, turn a weekly meeting into a meeting every two or four weeks, for example.

A good structure for brainstorming ideas around this is the 'What? So What? Now What?' liberating structure, [26] as per *The Surprising Power of Liberating Structures* by Henri Lipmanowicz and Keith McCandless. Particularly in a remote-only context, it helps pull out the beliefs,

---

[26] https://recommendedbyluke.com/WhatSoWhatNowWhat see https://recommendedbyluke.com/MiroWhatSoWhatNowWhat for an online whiteboard template.

assumptions, and meanings of specific meetings or meeting series. This is great input to help a team redesign a meeting that doesn't seem to be working.

Redesigning meetings

If the meeting needs to occur, but it's not achieving its purpose, then consider how you can redesign the meeting with these four areas: participants, structure, time, and relationships:

1. Who can be an optional participant? As a starting point, ask participants offline if they even want to attend. Most useful meetings have 3-4 participants. According to Wolf's sarcastic law of meetings, if there are more participants, the real decisions are probably being made elsewhere.
2. What the best "structure" for the meeting is, to engage on multiple levels. Ideally, you want everyone who shows up to engage. This includes either verbal or visual engagement with post-its and collaboratively edited documents.
3. How much time do you really need? Sometimes meetings are too short, and you only skim over the surface of underlying issues. If you get the sense that discussions are just starting to get interesting at the end of a half-hour meeting, you need 30 minutes for the group to build up enough context. Sometimes meetings are too long for what they're meant to

achieve. You don't need a workshop to figure out the color of company paperclips.
4. Consider how canceling a meeting could affect your working relationships with the participants. For example, if you cancel the only regular meeting you have with a senior stakeholder, you may find it harder to work with them in the future. They will lack the context the meeting provided.

Also, consider how you can apply this section's other tips to meetings. Look at the resources section and identify free or paid tools which you might find helpful when running this meeting. You may find it helpful to supplement this audit with detailed information on how you spent your time. Personal monitoring tools like RescueTime[27] and Rize[28] belong to a category of tools that monitor your computer usage to note down exactly how much time you spend on different tasks based on your app usage and web browsing activity. Currently, I am exploring Rize. It calculates the number of context switches I experience daily and weekly.

A home for every conversation

You can also use this spreadsheet to confront stakeholders if needed. Meetings are social by nature. Consider what kind of conversation happens in each meeting when

---

[27] https://www.rescuetime.com/
[28] https://rize.io/

establishing if the group should meet. Every meaningful conversation requires a home on your calendar.

To catch anything left over, you can try a Bullpen meeting [29] like the startup Coda. They have a scheduled time for ad hoc discussions. The Coda team batches topics together into a real-time agenda. A dedicated meeting cadence may be needed if a topic keeps being added to the bullpen.

What this means

When canceling meetings, you will win "additional" time to work. Don't waste time talking if you don't need it. Canceled meetings result in more unscheduled time. Employees want to deliver the promised results. Time is their key resource. When restructuring meetings, you have the opportunity to design the interaction from the ground up. What is the group's goal when getting together? What's keeping them from achieving it? How can the meeting be more fun? By improving your meetings, you indirectly improve your operating culture. Greater accountability for outcomes can only be a good thing.

Key takeaways

- Audit and prioritize the meetings you have for quality and quantity, and cancel any you can.

---

[29] https://recommendedbyluke.com/BullpenMeeting

- Redesign any important meetings or meeting flows, to maximize their usefulness while minimizing how much they distract participants.

Section takeaways

- While often vocally despised, meetings are complicated because they involve groups of people. They are an essential expression of company culture, in practice, and how most companies operate.
- When moving online, human interactions change significantly, especially during meetings.
- Pay attention to the following factors in your teams:
  - The participant's personal context changes when working outside the office. Look for clues in terms of how that changed context affects each person.
  - The meeting room or place in the office doesn't provide an implicit structure for a meeting, so alternative structures take their place, primarily based on the technology used to interact.
  - Choosing how you communicate will also dictate how important you think a particular discussion is.
- Spend at least as much time as the meeting preparing for it and structuring it. Then follow up afterward to make sure the decisions are implemented in practice.

Rethinking motivation

In which we deep dive into how to bring large groups of people together in order to act

Though each was partly in the right, and all were in the wrong! -John Godfrey Saxe

Quick challenge ideas

Following on with your success from the first round, here are a few quick challenges around your team's motivation. Didn't think it would be that easy, did you?

- Create an anonymous one form survey (use google forms if you don't have a standard company tool) that asks what the team is working on and why they are working on it. Send it to your team with a 24-hour deadline for response.
- Keep track of how many times per day you change tasks or change direction in terms of your attention. Share it with your team and suggest they try the same and share the results. It's enough to just have a piece of paper and a pen on your desk and notch down each time you shift direction. Count how many times this happens because of internal or external distractions, and how many times it's deliberate.

Why alignment is linked with motivation

The best way to think about remote work motivation, is to imagine each of your team's members is a volunteer. Treat it as a thought experiment. They come to work at your company for your team, because they are excited to work together with you. They could ply their trade, by working for your competition, and make approximately the same amount of money. [30] They are furthering their career, deepening their skills, and learning more about your industry.

Managers often assume that paying people and providing benefits should be enough. Studies show that pay increases affect happiness up to around $75k. This happiness may or may not spill over into job satisfaction. But in reality, there are other companies in your industry who would be happy to at least match the employee's current salary and benefits, if they needed to hire someone with experience. Your pay package doesn't differentiate you, everything else about your company does.

This is why it's helpful to adopt the high bar of managing

---

[30]While there may be differences in pay, these differences typically will not be life-changing differences for them. This is a common trap managers fall into, i.e. believing that money is the only motivator they have at their disposal.

volunteers to ensure that you're thinking about all factors influencing an individual's motivation. That's also why this thought experiment is useful: other than pay and benefits, how much of your attention do you spend on non-monetary reasons to engage with others and participate in their job?

To be honest, I had no idea how important and nuanced motivation was when I was completely new to being a manager. A young, local nonprofit where I volunteered was struggling. Membership was dwindling. The management team was arguing. And we were at risk of completely disappearing, if there wasn't enough participation. It was a classic bottom-up initiative. Initially everyone was enthusiastic, until eventually the incessant energy needed to sustain it started to weigh us down. Out of a sense of responsibility and not wanting to let it fizzle out, I agreed to step up. I didn't want the community around the organization to implode. I ran for president and won, because nobody else ran against me.

Upon taking the reins, I owned up and dove in. I mapped out the member acquisition process in Google sheets. I wanted to manage the end-to-end flow, from a potential member first hearing of us, to being deeply involved with the organization and its mission. I even mapped out metrics for each step of the process. In my mind, I'd chosen specific volunteer leaders, each of whom I expected to own a metric. I was keen to ensure that the organization continued to provide value systematically. I thought having a membership acquisition mapped out as a funnel would make it easier to diagnose where the key bottlenecks were.

When I presented my proposed approach to the volunteer functional leaders, they immediately rejected it. They didn't see a need for it, even though they were fully aware of the problems. Personally, I was flabbergasted. I was trying my best to prevent the current problems from continuing to happen. Yet they didn't see how my spreadsheet model would address those problems. In short, I failed to convince them when operationalizing the numeric model. More fundamentally, the problem was that it was my model, not our model.

"At the last monthly review, he lost a star performer to the Philly office"

To be fair, my effort wasn't entirely wasted. Throughout my presidency, the metrics served me as an early warning and informal quality control system. When I introduced changes to the organization later, I knew what was essential, thanks to my quantitative intuition about operations. I could articulate challenges by citing high-level numbers that I knew were critical to achieving the organization's mission.

This mishap served me well later when running teams professionally. I realized I tried to impose a top-down solution, sacrificing buy-in to solve the problem. Instead, I should've involved the team up front, at least enough for them to understand the implications of the problem, and let them come up with their own proposals.

As I gathered experience, I learned it was usually enough to articulate problems and their implications, as soon as I was aware of them. That was usually enough. The team went off and came up with solutions. The key difference was that they wanted to implement their solutions. They convinced themselves about their own ideas, so I didn't need to motivate them anymore. My primary role was to share perspectives, including my own, clarify implications for everyone, and articulate a goal together while mapping it onto everyone's individual motivation.

After that, team dynamics took over. And they motivated one another. They aligned.

Too many volunteers can be worse than too few

This mindset of thinking about your team as volunteers distills the key challenges of leadership: defining vision by framing the problem, delegating and coordinating work with clear priorities, balancing humility with courage, and so on.

If you want to reach people, you need to have a personal connection with them. Understand what they want. And help them understand how that fits into what's best for the group. Sometimes, the challenge isn't finding volunteers in crisis situations, like natural disasters or the beginning of a war. It's making sure that they are productive together, achieving what's most important together.

According to historian Yuval Noah Harari in his book *Sapiens*, humans dominated the world because we were the only animal that could cooperate flexibly in large numbers. This ability to create organizations was one of the core skills that made us uniquely successful as a species.

The most important aspect of this ability is to set clear priorities for a group, and then distribute those priorities in real-time. To adapt to opportunities and threats as they arise. An organization working towards a clear set of priorities, as well as the ability to change those priorities, will outperform competitors, build trust, and frankly will often be more fun to work for. And this state is called alignment. In this state, everyone is clear on what's expected of them. And if there is a team feeling that motivates everyone to contribute.

Alignment happens through conversation and dialogue about objectives, motivations and actions, and by exploring the disconnects among them. Given a large enough group of participants, there will be many disconnects. Some are accidental. Some are deliberate. All of them affect the company's ability to drive results.

So it's a full-time job for managers to diagnose these "disconnects". Aligning at all levels and deciding on a common goal is critical to enabling performance. After the company's attempt at alignment, what happens will depend on how clear-sighted everyone walked out of the alignment meeting, what they understood, and how well they mapped the goal onto immediate next tasks for themselves and their co-workers.

When achieved, alignment implies shared ownership around an objective. An emotional fuel powers the team or teams to achieve the objective. And actions align with that objective or intent, from the higher-level objective down to specific decisions and even in-the-moment tasks each team member performs.

Now go remote

When everyone lost the social context of the office, this remained. The ability of managers to connect with their teams and individuals by caring for them and helping them navigate intrusion of work-life into the home.

Companies had inadvertently outsourced their office space to employees, forcing them to scramble for a reasonable setup where they could be productive. It wasn't just a case of home office gear. If you didn't have a home office or a spare room to work, then your productivity plummeted.

Moreover, all of the stresses of work and home life spilled into one another. Suddenly, it mattered at work who was parenting rowdy and restless kids who had nothing to do. Schools and pre-schools were closed. This affected parent performance at work, and they had no realistic alternatives.

In this context, all soft skills needed to lead and coordinate volunteers became even more valuable. Management styles and company cultures assumed otherwise struggled and coped how they could.

As of 2022, Covid-19 still exists but doesn't affect work life as much as it did originally. The Economist reported that "Research by Nicholas Bloom of Stanford University suggests that, on average, employees reckon the blend of in-person and remote work is a perk equivalent to an 8% pay increase." At this point, hybrid or remote work is just an employee lifestyle trade-off.

Lack of alignment causes all kinds of problems

In the short term, it might not seem like a big deal, but eventually, alignment affects operating profits and company effectiveness.

Here's a quick taste of how misalignment looks and feels:

- Increases anxiety
- Adds confusion
- Abates learning
- Reduces performance
- Decreases engagement
- Increases employee turnover

In short, it kills motivation, which affects most human factors in a company. The financial implications of alignment will largely depend on how expensive employee turnover is for you. In industries where payroll makes up a significant chunk of operating costs, like construction or IT, this impact is even more drastic.

Unfortunately, by the time your employees announce their resignation, it's too late to take action. Often employee turnover is not tied to the root cause of the problem. These can include factors like unclear outcomes, poor delegation, and accountability. Or there may be other reasons.

Sadly, this is common. Many studies around employee engagement paint the picture. Gallup is the most famous one, where roughly 70% of employees are "disengaged" or "actively disengaged" in their job. And it's been so every year for 30+ years, at thousands of blue-chip companies. Keeping this in mind, I knew I had to prioritize and monitor engagement when looking to improve team effectiveness. I wanted to free up my teams to do meaningful work and to feel more engaged with what they are paid to do. I find it tragic that 70% of employees work for years on jobs they don't like, just going through the motions.

Initially, I wasn't sure how. As a manager of remote teams, I initially spent my time fighting operational fires. If there was any crisis, usually there was some kind of bottleneck at the root of that crisis. Once the fires died down, I realized we could also identify and remove bottlenecks to achieve our outcomes faster. If there wasn't a crisis, the best way to increase productivity was to identify areas of friction which had become bottlenecks affecting my team.

Key takeaways

- Alignment helps your teams stay effective and motivated, both of which are big challenges when working remotely.
- A useful incremental measure of alignment: how much the team members and leaders give the same responses to questions around the why, what, and how of what they're working on.
- If successfully aligned, a team feels an emotional fuel, powering the teams to achieve strategic objectives.

- Alignment and culture are strongly related, and a lack of alignment in a remote first world will cause employees to disengage and leave for greener remote pastures elsewhere.

How to reduce ambiguity and why it matters

> A traveler came upon three men who were laboring.
>
> He asked the first man what he was doing, and the man said he was laying bricks and would be glad at the end of the day.
>
> He asked the second man the same question, and he said he was putting up a wall and was tired and eager for the workday to end.
>
> He got to the third man, and he asked him the same question, but this man looked up smiling and said, "I'm building a cathedral."
>
> source: unknown

This parable illustrates the importance of meaning when thinking about motivation.

The key role of leadership is assigning meaning and therefore choosing what is essential and why. In the ideal case, a leader captures the imagination of the whole organization, where they all understand they are building a cathedral, and not just laying bricks.

Assigning meaning this way resolves ambiguity. Here, ambiguity refers to how the same "thing" can be interpreted in multiple ways. For example, each person in the same company will understand the importance of an event, like an IT system malfunction, differently. Consider the importance of the employee's role. A salesperson will consider the impact on their expected bonus. A developer will think it's an interesting puzzle it stopped working right now. In addition to role, if the company strategy is pulling in different directions, each direction will also map to why certain people care, depending on what they're involved in.

Ambiguity results in a lack of clarity because of multiple interpretations of the current state of a company. Each participant has a slightly different context. In an organization, ambiguity occurs on an individual, functional, departmental, project or any other level that includes any subgroup in a company. Each subgroup will have a shared interpretation of any circumstances the company finds itself in. These interpretations are context dependent, i.e. if the environment changes, then opinions and interpretations can change.

In practice, leaders set or discover priorities in order to reduce ambiguity. Setting and pursuing priorities happens socially within the company. Conversation, interaction, and relationships are where this happens:

> A significant portion of the organizational en-

> vironment consists of nothing more than talk, symbols, promises, lies, interest, attention, threats, agreements, expectations, memories, rumors, indicators, supporters, detractors, faith, suspicion, trust, appearances, loyalties, and commitments. (Weick 1985)

As this happens mostly verbally, it can occur on a zoom call just as well as in person. And it does.

The basic implication of operational ambiguity: everyone sees something slightly different, thus making it difficult to "reason" about it together consistently. To make sense of it together. At the same time, if there are multiple competing interpretations, each interpretation can be a source of interruption and distraction.

The net result of this ambiguity is that employees are context-switching among priorities that shift constantly. This shows up in various ways: starting projects with too small of a scope to accomplish anything, sacrificing quality because of a new priority. In short, it's difficult to complete meaningful work. Each 'boss' has a different definition of what's meaningful, and pulls in his or her own direction. Priorities are continuously re-ordered, based on who has the most influence at the moment.

When this happens, the key questions that emerge are:

- How do you coordinate action with multiple overlapping subjective realities?
- What is the "distribution of interruption" in organizations?

- How does being remote affect this largely verbal process?

How you answer these questions will determine your effectiveness as a remote leader, and therefore how happy your immediate boss (and ultimately your customer) eventually becomes.

The leader's role

The key role of a leader is the reduction of distraction through clearly articulated priorities and implications. Leader effectiveness lies in the ability of the leader to give others a sense of what they are doing and to articulate this sense so the participants can communicate about the meaning of their behavior. If done well, this inspires and motivates.

First and foremost, the leader defines the frame, reducing ambiguity and simplifying expectations. "Leadership lies in large part in generating a point of reference, against which a feeling of organization and direction can emerge" (Smirchich and Morgan). In more practical terms, this point of reference is what author Jim Collins calls a Big Hairy Audacious Goal (BHAG) in *Good to Great*.

The classic example here is JFK's putting a man on the moon by the end of the 1960s. On the surface, this was just a goal for the US space program. In practice, though, this goal articulated what mattered relative to international relations, particularly with the USSR's take on the space race. It caught everyone's imagination, including regular people who voted for him. Within NASA, it served as a pithy reference point for all decisions: which option will help or not detract from that reference point?

For a more current example, I suspect Facebook's push to the Metaverse in October 2021 may eventually land in this category. Initially, I thought "metaverse" and VR was more of a clever PR ploy to distract from the current regulatory woes of the company. But after hearing founder Mark Zuckerberg speak about what Facebook is actually doing on Tim Ferriss' podcast, it genuinely sounds like an attempt to pursue a risky long-term vision that could change how we live and we work.

The immediate result of a clearly articulated vision is the reduction of ambiguity. Only one interpretation becomes meaningful. Once it's clear to the company what is most meaningful, it's much easier to act. Direction is unambiguous. It helps focus all resources and attention on attaining that chosen reference point.

Problem-setting as a core leadership skill

Once the frame is defined, priorities are the next level down for aspiring leaders. They serve as a filtering mechanism, first and foremost. By committing to a top priority, after deciding it would have the greatest expected benefit among alternatives, the leader helps the company filter out everything else.

The operations challenge is two-fold in this context. First determine what the priority is. Then filter out everything else until it's accomplished, without constantly re-assessing it. Usually the top priority involves addressing the most valuable problem, opportunity, or risk facing the company at the moment. A goal is merely an attempt to satisfy an identified need. Once the top priority or problem is resolved, there is another one on the list. The work of a leader is knowing about all potential problems, assigning each one meaning, and prioritizing them effectively.

Problem-setting is how effective leaders motivate their teams on a day-to-day basis, to address the top priority challenge. Problem-setting usually requires an intuitive grasp of context, in order to set and communicate the problem effectively. A well-set problem motivates everyone associated to go solve it. Before you go ahead and solve problems and achieve goals, you need to have a very clear understanding of the challenge. Typically, companies are in such a rush that employees don't give themselves the space to define the problem precisely, both customer or internal company problems.

Ideally, problems or challenges are quantified by **choosing key metrics to express the problem, and a clear set of actions can be taken to move those key metrics.** This way, they frame the company agenda. If top leadership is tempted to get in and solve problems themselves, that takes away the pleasure and ownership of the problem from the people who most need to act on it. Their time is better spent investigating and prioritizing problems to be solved. If problems aren't being addressed, they aren't articulated precisely enough for the people who need to do the work. While it's tempting to treat problem setting as a communication technique, it requires effort, thinking, and creativity to frame the problem effectively so that it's clear why it's a "burning platform" for everyone involved.

For major challenges, problem setting needs to occur at every layer of the company to identify the correct root causes. For example, author Michael Lewis talks about the bumpy go-live of healthcare.gov the L6 episode of his podcast "Against the Rules". [31]

The website was managed by a large external agency. All of the senior leaders and the Obama administration knew the site was an embarrassing problem. It wasn't until the person who stepped up to solve the problem got 6 levels down, when speaking to the external contractors actually managing the site, that he found someone who understood the technical issues and had ideas for fixing this. Once these suggestions were introduced back to the top of the company, the problem was fixed.

The fewer priorities there are, the easier it is to determine if any given person contributes to that priority. To hold yourself accountable for that priority. Ideally, everyone is focused on one top priority or supporting the people working on it. The classic example here is Steve Jobs returning to Apple in 1997 when it was in a moment of existential crisis. He cut the product line down from 31

---

[31] https://recommendedbyluke.com/L6Lewis

down to 4, with one product for each major market in which he wanted to compete. The starting point was the market segments: already robust demand that was growing rapidly. As a result, this reduced complexity thanks to filtering in what was important, laid the groundwork for building Apple into the behemoth it is today.

Also, priorities help the company establish a "relationship with the goal," as discussed in Gary Keller's book *The One Thing*. If something is truly important it should be performed regularly, with processes that ensure forward progress. There should be resources allocated. There should be timeboxes to pursue that priority. It should be mapped down to daily activities for which different individuals hold themselves responsible. Just declaring something is a priority, e.g. strategy by PowerPoint, has limited value if that strategy isn't explicitly applied to daily operations, decisions, and trade-offs.

Why ambiguity reduction matters (so much)

The emotional impact of ambiguity on employees is less obvious. If everyone is working from the same frame and they're focused on the same problems with the same objective constraints, there is much less conflict and confusion. It doesn't matter which "subgroup" or tribe(s) you belong to within a company. With less ambiguity, employees are less distracted. They are less stressed. They are more focused. They aren't interrupted by an unexpected change in someone's agenda. And as a result, the subjective level of emotional arousal is more conducive to great achievement.

Interruptions hit us at our most primordial level, disorienting us. In terms of time frames, this happens at the level of neuroception, as defined by Stephen Porges in his masterpiece *The Polyvagal Theory*. Neuroceptive reactions occur in milliseconds before people are consciously aware that they will be reacting. These reactions occur in the lowest, oldest layers of the brain, *before* they reach the emotional and the cognitive parts of the brain. For example, The commonly cited stat among programmers is that it typically takes around 25-30 minutes to get back into creative flow when we are distracted out of it. Interruptions disrupt the automatic processes in our bodies and brain. The autonomous nervous system gets aroused, and then responds habitually with a fight, flight, or freeze response–disrupting any previously existing state. Then it causes an emotional reaction, and an attempt to "cognitively" make sense of the interruption. When this whole process completes, the person can continue where they left off.

Karl Weick summarizes why this matters in his classic *Sensemaking in Organizations*. Arousal is triggered by interruptions of ongoing activity. The perception of arousal triggers a rudimentary act of sensemaking, even if it's involuntary. It warns of a stimulus. The interrupted person must pay attention, in case the interruption requires immediate action (fight, flight, freeze). Usually, the emotional arousal happens 2-3 seconds after being triggered. Once in a state of arousal, people try to construct some link between the present state and "relevant" prior situations to make sense of it. [32]

Interruption is a signal that important changes have occurred in the environment, either negative or positive. Thus, a key event sparking emotion is the "interruption of an expectation". In a highly ambiguous environment, competing agendas of different sheriffs within a company mean that people lower down in the hierarchy are constantly interrupted, spending most of their attention in that dazed 30-minute state. They're slowly coming back into flow. Frequently, they are interrupted again before they reach it. As a result, they often feel like they're in a state of "danger", as opposed to psychological safety. (More on psychological safety later)

Not to villainize interruptions completely, some of them cause a positive emotional response, according to Weick. Two professional examples would include:

- Removal of an expected negative stimulus.
- Unexpected acceleration of a plan or behavior sequence.

If a piece of work completes ahead of schedule, it could also be an interruption of sorts—a good one that makes you want to celebrate.

---

[32] Berscheid (1983) and Mandler (1984) focus on the interruption of standard operating procedures, or effectively organizational habits, that exist to make things happen efficiently and without the need for additional strategic input.

If you expect a tedious bit of work to come up, but you learn that a new IT system feature has automated it away, it affects you similarly.

Ironically, both of these happen more frequently in environments with clear priorities and well-framed problems. If you and all your colleagues are only working on the top priority, it gets done quickly. Often quicker than expected, because you don't need to coordinate efforts and give context to pull another stakeholder in.

The key role of leadership, especially in a larger organization, is ambiguity reduction. This is done by setting the right frame and then consistently problem setting. If done successfully, everyone in the company (including themselves) will be less frequently interrupted, and more likely to experience psychological flow and peak performance. They experience the joy of missing out, by being able to dive deeply into high-priority work without distraction.

Key takeaways

- A leader's key responsibility is the reduction of ambiguity within a company, which can be done both in-person or remotely as it's largely based on conversation and communication.
- Frame setting, prioritization, and problem setting are three key techniques that reduce ambiguity.
- If done correctly, you minimize the amount of time employees spend in a distracted (and emotionally aroused) state.

Forests, trees, and motivation

> Speaker 1 (00:05) I've developed a chemical isomer that links to volatile organic compounds, causing carbon bonds to rupture and wraps them in a nanotube coating.
>
> Speaker 2 (00:14) Huh. That's a little confusing. Can you dumb it down for me?
>
> Speaker 1 (00:19) Sure. What I do is I take a proprietary isomer that I developed with a picric acid wash that hollows out the carbon bonds and replaces them with a nanotube wrapping.
>
> Speaker 2 (00:31) Okay, so I guess it's pretty technical.
>
> source: hugeshoesale [a]
> ---
> [a]https://recommendedbyluke.com/WhyHowGap

In a nutshell, this gently humorous interaction illustrates exactly what a lack of context in a discussion is like. Everyone is an expert in their little corner of a company, their silo. In a company, each employee has their equivalent of a "chemical isomer that links to volatile organic compounds". They're the sole expert on the "how" of a particular topic: engineering, payroll, HR, etc. They are so focused on exactly how things work in their area that they might miss the wider "why" behind the work. To be effective as an employee, you need to understand how your work relates to everyone else's work.

As a leader, you own and steward your team's context. Context invites each team member to identify what is valuable, to engage, and to create value together. And what was lost when the world's office was sent home? Context. And with that context? Clarity, motivation, and engagement also went out the window in many cases.

"Why" is excellent as an exploratory tool in that it tends to be inclusive. Answers can often be understood by anyone instead of "how", requiring detailed expertise in a particular field. In *The Art of Explanation*, Lee Lefever argues why and how exist on a spectrum. Why is meant to be something anyone can understand, whereas the further you get into the "how", the more you need specialized knowledge and for someone to geek out. For example, engineering academics can get deep into the how with their peers, but for a lay audience, the "why" behind their work is all that matters. If they jump deep into explaining how something works, they will lose almost everyone.

The same is true across functional areas in a company. It's not necessary for a software developer to understand how accounts receivable work in detail, but they should be able to understand why there is an accounts receivable department, and what a person working there wants. This enables both sides to negotiate a mutually beneficial arrangement, and aligns their interests.

> People don't have to agree with each other. Seeking agreement creates disruption and a lot of unnecessary meetings. Instead, find a higher purpose around which people can align, even if they disagree on how to attain that purpose. [a]
>
> [a] from the 2018 innovator's handbook: https://recommendedbyluke.com/InnovatorsHandbook

For this reason, using "why" to explore problems establishes a common mental model for everyone involved in the discussion. Suppose they need a more detailed understanding of how, they will know who to ask. And everyone understands the big picture enough to be able to start coming up with a solution.

Moreover, there are usually mixed levels of context in any interaction on a given topic, such as a kickoff meeting. Each department forms its own context. Each type of expertise. Each person has a unique perspective and notices different details. There can be mixed levels of documentation or previous feedback. You need to establish the same context and explain the context. As a team lead, Lee LeFever suggests that you consider the following questions in *The Art of Explanation*:

- How do you find the right amount of context?
- How do you estimate the audience's existing knowledge?

- How do you impress both the experts AND the beginners?

For example, think of a zoom room of ten people with a mix of existing expertise in a topic. A few will share your level of expertise. Most will have a passing knowledge of the topic or purpose of the call. And some will have no idea, because they are too high or low in the company hierarchy. To help everyone feel confident, it can be enough to spend a few sentences or minutes establishing the context of the discussion, so that everyone understands why the meeting is happening. Or why this topic is essential. This helps them feel confident enough to follow the conversation or interaction as it happens, even if they don't understand every implementation or technical detail.

Start with the forest, then go into the trees. Lee LeFever says "Done well, context makes it possible to invite experts and beginners alike to see ideas from a new, helpful perspective."

Establishing context is a critical leadership skill. Everyone in the company can ask why something is important or needed. If the experts don't understand the broader context, the organization will likely be ineffective. The how is not tied to why, to the company's larger purpose.

How to leverage individuals' natural motivation, by connecting it to the larger why

Probably the most critical skill of a manager is the ability to link up an individual's natural motivation to the bigger picture. Luna and Renninger call it a Linkup in their managerial skills book *The Leader Lab*: "The Linkup is the explicit connection of an action to its goal." All too often, activity, i.e., being or even looking busy, is prioritized over actually getting something useful done. It's much better to be certain that any activity undertaken helps achieve something the company values and wants.

Probe your team members for the intended impact, benefit, and outcome in a given "how", to make it explicit. This surfaces assumptions and helps you coordinate effort while respecting the motivation and engagement people are already bringing to the table. Then you won't need to manipulate them into feeling motivated later.

Alternatively, articulate a decision rule that communicates the strategic intent. "If your team members know that the conference they're planning links up to increasing sales leads by 20% (while keeping conference costs below $100K), they can make decisions on their own without constantly checking in with you about everything from ticket costs to napkin colors. The Linkup becomes the ultimate guide for decision-making rather than the manager." This way, you don't need to micro-manage the details of how the conference is being organized; employees get the autonomy to figure it out for themselves, while you still achieve the best possible outcome for your company.

The linkup can also be a tool for self-management. Indeed, Luna and Renninger claim that the best managers often asked Linkup questions of themselves. Being clear on whether you are working on an important goal and allowing yourself to lean into that is an excellent tool to achieve what matters quickly.

Conversely, you can dig into why the team member is passionate or excited about something, in order to figure out their natural flow strategy, as per Diane Allen. This helps you understand how to support that person effectively, while also laying the groundwork for eventually getting the entire team in a sustained "flow" state. She likens this to the chemical process behind the ripening of apples:

> In order to understand how this works in a group situation, let's take a look at biology. How do positive feedback loops function in biology? ... When an apple is exposed to the gas ethylene, it ripens. But when the apple ripens, it releases the gas ethylene. Now, all of the apples around it are exposed to that [apple]. Then they will ripen and because of this, apple trees are known to ripen all at the same time. So instead of a chain reaction, it's exponential. So when you get one person in their flow state, they all get into flow.

Allen used her insight from leading the orchestra to orchestrate the musicians into creative group flow...predictably. Having a solid understanding of what happens when individuals get into flow can help everyone achieve more in the same amount of time.

Asking 'Why' guides you to root causes of problems

Asking why forces you to find the root of the problem and permits you to explore where the problem lies in the wider company. Identify root causes –with a goal in mind.

The Old English poem of Grendel illustrates the power of why. Grendel the monster terrorized the countryside, and a local lord named Hrothgar challenged his warriors to slay the beast offering untold riches. Beowulf, a warrior from a neighboring tribe, steps up and volunteers to address the problem. While Beowulf self-promotes and pounds his chest while getting drunk in a mead hall, Grendel creeps in. Being unarmed, Beowulf swallows his pride and wrestles Grendel to the death, tearing off Grendel's arm in the process. Later he uses it as a trophy in the mead hall. Hrothgar celebrates Beowulf's victory, but unfortunately, that's not the full story. Not long after Grendel dies, Grendel's mother comes to wreak revenge on these pesky humans, and does a pretty good job. Beowulf and his clansmen chase her down into a cave below a swamp where she lives. Initially, he tries the same approach as he did with Grendel and engages in hand-to-hand combat, but almost loses his life doing so.

> 'Mid the battle-gear saw he a blade triumphant,
>
> old-sword of Eotens, with edge of proof,
>
> warriors' heirloom, weapon unmatched,
>
> – save only 'twas more than other men
>
> to bandy-of-battle could bear at all –
>
> as the giants had wrought it, ready and keen.
>
> Seized then its chain-hilt the Scyldings' chieftain,
>
> bold and battle-grim, brandished the sword,
>
> reckless of life, and so wrathfully smote
>
> that it gripped her neck and grasped her hard,
>
> her bone-rings breaking: the blade pierced through
>
> that fated-one's flesh: to floor she sank.

Now that he was at the bottom of the swamp, he resourcefully found and grabbed a sword lying there, and used it to stab and defeat Grendel's Mother.

Other than being a great monster story from high school English classes, this story illustrates the importance of going after root causes of problems. Of thinking through why you have the problem in the first place. It stresses that you often need to go to the bottom of the proverbial swamp to address root causes, which often isn't pleasant.

When you truly commit to addressing the root causes of problems, you find what you need to fully address them on your path, like the old sword of Eotens. And finally, it requires deep focus and intensity, ideally with the support of your co-worker tribe, to make sure that this problem goes away permanently.

At this point, you are exploring the full depth of problems and, more importantly, their root causes.

- Why did this mini-[crisis] happen exactly?
- Why are we doing X in the first place?
- Does it make sense to continue doing so?
- Should we do why?
- What are we trying to achieve, exactly?

One great tool for this in a workshop or other interactive format is the Lean "5 Why" exercise. After a problem occurs, gather together the affected people. It's important to stress that the inquiry is being made in a safe space, especially emotionally. You want to improve life at work for everyone, not to hang those responsible. Using a neutral or friendly tone, ask the affected individuals why it occurred. Then ask why that happened. And again. And again. Keep asking until you get to the root cause. Once you have a root cause, ask the group how this can be prevented in the future. What can you change as a team or as a company, in order to make sure it doesn't happen again?

The core of every question at this stage is "why?". This is a question everyone will understand, and it doesn't require a Ph.D. to understand the root drivers of a situation. To solve the problem, it should be described in terms that anyone—even a small child—can understand. Or even the guys from payroll. And everyone agrees that this is a problem.

A clear "Why" improves your ability to delegate

Why are "Whys" so important to managers? Even if you don't have a great reason why providing some justification for a request is a good practice for leaders to follow. There is a classic office copier study [33] around the impact of using why to justify a request. In it, strangers are standing in a queue to photocopy documents. Someone comes in and tries to butt in and jump the queue 120 times using three different strategies:

1. "Excuse me, I have 5/20 pages. May I use the xerox machine?"
2. "Excuse me, I have 5/20 pages. May I use the xerox machine, because I have to make copies?"
3. "Excuse me, I have 5/20 pages. May I use the xerox machine, because I am in a rush?"

The first formulation of the request is the baseline, where no reason why is provided. In the second case, the reason provided is not adding any new information on top of the

---

[33] https://recommendedbyluke.com/CopierWhy

same request as the first option. Finally, the last wording offers additional context and information as to why this request is justified.

nr. of pages	no info	placebo info	sufficient info
5	60%	93%	94%
20	20%	24%	42%

Giving a legitimate reason for the request provides the best results, but giving a poor reason is more effective than not giving any reason at all. This digs into mindless, pre-rational, automatic behavior we all have as humans. As the request got larger, providing a proper justification outperformed the other two approaches.

As leaders, it's safe to say that explicitly justifying all requests you make is a great habit. This includes work that is delegated. Ideally, the reason you provide is genuinely why you believe the task needs to be done. But even if it isn't, the brain's natural tendency is to increase compliance to requests from others with an attached justification.

It's safe to say that the behavioral effect of justifying your requests is location-independent. It works when everyone involved is working remotely, possibly even more so given the limited social contact with co-workers.

Why is powerful, but it can piss people off

As a directly posed question, "why" feels intense. It can put the listener on the defensive back heel, particularly if they feel their judgment or person is being questioned. Chris Voss, an FBI hostage negotiator, noticed this reaction. In a tense standoff, you don't have much room for friendly root cause inquiry. It can trigger unnecessary conflict, particularly if the person questioned is already emotionally aroused.

Pay attention to how Why questions land at work, and look for alternative ways to ask for the same thing. For example, Carole Stizza, the author of *The Ask Framework*, says:

> When you ask somebody the question of 'why', like, why aren't you showing up? Why aren't you speaking up in the meeting? Why aren't you on the video? It makes people go backward in their brains and defend their choices. It doesn't allow the conversation to go forward…'how' and 'what' and 'how to move forward' questions [are better]. How would you like to see me engage you in the meeting? What would you like me to ask you so that I get your expertise on this topic?

Try to probe around, using what and how questions to unearth the underlying reasons. Propose something. If your ideas are rejected, then look for an underlying pattern. Then ask about the pattern. People often find it easier to explain what they don't want or why they don't want something rather than explain what they want.

Also, forward-facing questions like "How do we...?" effectively diffuse difficult situations than backward-facing "Why?". This is in line with the feed-forward approach proposed by Jeffrey Pfeffer in his book *Power*: "when people focus on what they need to get to the next stage of their careers, they are less defensive." This is primarily about framing feedback or problem-solving in a way that diffuses tense situations.

In short, the context and tone of asking "Why" can matter significantly. Pay attention so that it doesn't blow up in your face.

Summary

Continuously connecting the why and how in a company make purpose and outcomes clear: of meetings, of tasks, etc... at every level of the company. It also makes sure that employees are clear on what needs to happen, and how that ties into what they are already interested in.

Key takeaways

- Why is inclusive in a company context, as everyone can understand and discuss work at this level,

regardless of their functional area or level in the company hierarchy.
- A core habit effective managers repeatedly practice is the Linkup, where they explicitly link what should be done and how it should be done with why it matters. The most common challenge employees have is that they don't see how high level company goals relate to their day-to-day efforts.
- Use Why questions to investigate and eliminate root causes of problems.
- Providing a reason why something needs to be done increases the persuasiveness of the request and the likelihood it will happen.
- Asking why too frequently can be perceived as aggressive and can backfire potentially. It may be better to use 'how' questions in order to address problematic behaviors in this context.

Why context drives people

> **Scientist:** "My findings are meaningless if taken out of context."
>
> 15 minutes later...
>
> **AP Newswire and Google News:** Scientist claims his findings are meaningless

The physical experience of working remotely is markedly different from walking around the office among meeting rooms, sitting in a cubicle, or occasionally pulling up a chair in the boardroom. One of the side effects of moving to a remote-only culture across all companies is that everyone has the same physical experience of working from home:

- At your desk
- On your couch with a smartphone and potato chips
- Having a call across seven time zones while picking up your kids
- Zooming from your car, parked in front of the post office

Regardless of who you work for as an employee, the above experience will be the same. Everyone proverbially plugs into the "Matrix" every morning and unplugs in the evening.

The physical experience is an example of context. And context affects our judgment, especially with respect to other people.

remote work also happens on a whitespace background

The effect is similar to the visual impact of seeing sci-fi characters enter VR and only have their character on a solid white background. The impact of their body language is amplified many times, because there is no backdrop. Low context is like this stock photo whitespace. It amplifies or distorts the importance or value of what you do see, with a greater focus on what's visible.

What is context?

Erin Meyer's book, *The Culture Map* analyzes and classifies real-world cultures globally according to eight different "variables". Context sensitivity was one of those eight. In a nutshell, the context between two people is the difference between going on a first date (low context) vs. being married for 50 years (high context). Virtual culture and online interactions are very "low context" by default.

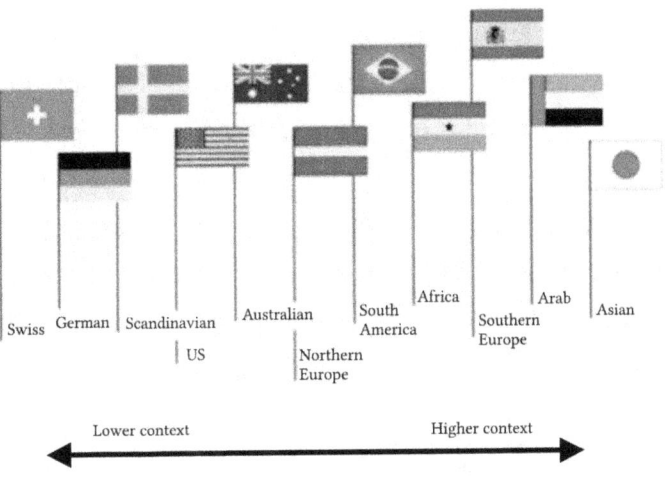

real-world cultures mapped by context

Low context refers to cultures that presume very little and typically value directness and clarity when interacting with others. The US is a good example of a relatively low-context culture. Built on the culture of accepting immigrants, America values being explicit and not making assumptions when speaking with others. It's safe to assume they might have completely different values than you.

This is easier to understand in relative terms: Polish culture was roughly in the middle regarding the importance of context compared to cultures globally. For example, when my Polish parents first moved to the US, they were bothered by how loudly people spoke. In a traditional Polish context, being loud is considered impolite, if not crude and arrogant. In the US, speaking loudly communicates confidence in yourself and in what you are saying. They also didn't feel comfortable "educating" the Americans because it was "obvious" (to them) that the Americans' behavior was unpleasant. Coming from a largely homogenous country, they fell into the trap of assuming that everyone shared their context. In their home country, that was true. In American culture, it wasn't. In the US, if someone's behavior bothers you, you are expected to be assertive, say something and negotiate with others. Both approaches are neither wrong or right; context dictates which one is appropriate.

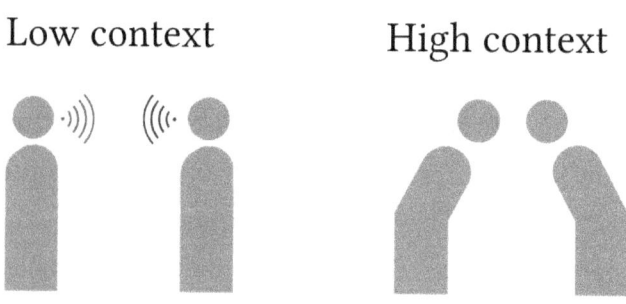

how people expect you to communicate

Going to the other extreme, an example of an extremely high context culture is Japan. Even though Japan is demographically homogenous, according to Meyer, the Japanese focus on collective harmony far above the relatively individualistic approaches common in Europe or the US. Moreover, most communication happens in subtexts, symbols, and cultural references. These symbols are shared among themselves, but they aren't particularly clear for anyone outside their culture, even other Asian cultures like the Chinese. The Japanese value being able to communicate a lot of "messages" in short amounts of "content". The shared cultural and historical context packs a lot more meaning into every message they send among themselves. The Japanese expect a high signal-to-noise ratio in all communication. They actively look for hidden or implied meanings when speaking with or writing to each other.

High context helps describe the attractiveness of working from the office. Working from the office provided social and cultural context. In this sense, company culture naturally existed in the office. Physically going to work meant changing to a company context, similar to traveling to another country. When everyone started working from home, most employees felt they lost social connection with their co-workers. But if their company culture wasn't already low context-in order to be inclusive of remote workers or employees distributed in various offices, they felt lost.

Why context matters

Context is critical in understanding what drives people and why they act (or not). On one hand, individual traits tend to be the typical way of understanding people's behavior. Sally is an extrovert. Bob is judgmental. Personality tests like Myers-Briggs, or hundreds of different corporate personality assessments, give insight into inherent personality traits and what they mean for that person when working in a group. On its own, in various benchmarking studies, traits explain only about 30% of a specific person's behavior, according to Todd Rose in *The End of Average*

> "When it comes to predicting the behavior of individuals—as opposed to predicting the average behavior of a group of people—traits actually do a poor job. In fact, correlations between personality traits and behaviors that should be related—such as aggression and getting into fights, or extroversion and going to parties—are rarely stronger than 0.30. Just how weak is that? According to the mathematics of correlation, it means that **your personality traits explain 9 percent of your behavior.**" [34]

On the other hand, behavior and expectations depend a lot on context. Certain conversation topics like religion are typically off-limits if you are at work because they can be unnecessarily divisive in a larger company. But it would be perfectly ok to discuss religion at home with friends or at church, synagogue, or mosque. So, in fact, you exhibit both behaviors. Surprisingly the same is true of many traits tested for in personality assessment. At best, personality testing gives you a reading "on average", but it doesn't explain how you behave most of the time. Not every behavior or reaction is context-specific, or we'd

---
[34] Rose, Todd. The End of Average

all be behaving exactly the same way when our immediate context changes. More importantly, this reading isn't accurate enough (at 9%) to use as the sole basis for business and team decisions like hiring, promoting, etc.

That said, there is something consistent about our identity, even though it's not our traits. Yuichi Shoda discovered that we are behaviorally consistent within a given context. It's not traits or context. Behavior emerges out of the interaction between them. The combination of traits and context give you a much better ability to understand and forecast individual behavior than either factor on its own.

In his book *The Person in Context*, Shoda suggested the use of what he calls "If-then signatures" to help understand what drives people. IF I am working from home, THEN I feel lonely and become extroverted. If I am working from an open plan office, the noisy hum intimidates me, and I am introverted. IF I am working from home AND the kids are home, THEN I am easily angered. But the opposite might be true for my colleague, Ben. If Ben is working from home AND his kids are home, THEN he feels pleased to connect with his kids throughout the day AND is more chatty than usual on work calls.

Context provides meaning and purpose; clarity of purpose is very important when working in teams. Online interactions are low context, therefore, making it difficult to achieve together if you don't know and apply the strategies for working in "low context". When online, the primary context is driven by what is easily observed when sitting at your desk: your objectives, KPIs, and the apps on your screen. This is the lens through which you analyze individual data points or events as they happen. It's up to you as a manager and an employee to use that context to figure out what matters using that context instead of the in-office one you had earlier. There will always be more stuff to keep you busy. According to author Perry Marshall, the "#1 success skill of the 21st century is the ability to identify the 'vital few' factors that matter." And context drives how you prioritize because context gives meaning to what you do.

Work context

A remote meeting participant's context is not a work context by default. It's a personal one. Because work integrates fluidly with personal concerns, the context for each person is quite different at the beginning of every meeting.

Not only did the context change for previously in-office employees, but for many, it changed into a hostile one in the short term. For example, experienced presenters suddenly feel pushed out of their depth. As they yammer away, the audience with whom they had eye contact and body language feedback in real-time are now having the following external experience, as remote presentations expert Dean Waye relates:

> "A messy room, kids in the dining room at the

> dining table. Your wife or husband is doing their own zoom call, and just walking around because they're doing it on their phone. 'Get out of here! I'm trying to be on my call.' [These are] noises and events that wouldn't be happening if we were all in a little conference room somewhere with ten chairs in it."

At the start of a meeting, you need to pull every person into the topic at hand. They don't have the cue of strolling into the company boardroom to start thinking about what needs to be done.

The Trello team articulated this problem well in their remote work guide: [35]

> When you're communicating digitally, you never quite know what the other person is doing at that moment. They might be at their desk just like you are, or they may be frantically rushing to a sales meeting, only responding "Yes" to your question and not elaborating because they don't have time. Without understanding the other person's context, you might think that person doesn't care about the issue you brought up.... With the information on that person's context, all of a sudden, the curt answers make sense: It's not that your co-worker doesn't care, they are just indisposed at the moment.

---

[35] https://recommendedbyluke.com/TrelloRemote

In practice, this has meant that employees needed to reallocate part of their personal living space to work concerns. Until they had clear boundaries and a space to work from home, their productivity suffered. And often this wasn't possible, as you can't add another room to an apartment or house overnight, if at all.

Internal context

Finally, each participant has an internal context, particularly for teams involved in analytical or creative "white-collar" work. For me personally, this became evident using a meditative time management technique called Pomodoro Technique.[36] You set a kitchen timer for blocks of 25 minutes allocated to individual tasks one at a time. Then, you take 5 minute breaks between each block of time. If a distraction occurs, you mark it down on a sheet of paper. The tracking sheet helps you differentiate between an external interruption, like a spouse walking up to ask a question, and an internal one, where your attention drifts off to something other than the immediate task at hand, like a ball game on the weekend. It's a type of focused deep work which feels uncomfortable, precisely because it draws your attention to how much your internal distractions are preventing you from making meaningful progress.

Investor philosopher Paul Graham penned a classic essay [37] on the fundamental dichotomy of how an ideal

---

[36] https://recommendedbyluke.com/Pomodoro

[37] https://recommendedbyluke.com/MakerManagerSchedule

maker calendar looks, vs. how an ideal manager calendar looks. Makers need big blocks of uninterrupted quiet time and minimal distractions. Managers, in contrast, work through people, and much of that happens at meetings. So unlike makers, they don't view meetings as a distraction; it's their bread and butter. The main takeaway from this essay was the importance of minimizing distractions, including internal ones, so that makers and the actual team responsible for doing the work can be productive.

When you don't have the social context of in-office meetings, the relative impact of these internal interruptions increases even during meetings. If a meeting forces you to sit in one place and stare passively at a screen while consuming information, the internal interruptions can cause you to only remember a few minutes from the entire hour. We are up against our biological limitations, ones that come from the physical structure of our brains. For this reason, the purpose, the design, and the emotional experience of meetings come to the fore. It's a lot more important to keep presentations short, e.g., ten minutes in one go, with non-presentation content or a break on either end. It's hard to stay focused for longer on abstract and complicated material in one shot, especially in a remote context.

In the next section, we'll go through types of context that can cause people to act or decide differently than they did when you worked together in the office.

Company context

Once you consider work and internal context, the company itself is a unique and essential context. For one, the company serves certain customer segments and provides specific products. For another, each person's position in a company serves as a really important context that influences everything else they notice and value.

External metrics

For example, at the strategic and operational level, you'll find all of the below significantly impact decisions made by everyone in the company.

1. Expected customer impact <-the big one
2. Opportunity size
3. Competition:
4. Channels: how are we reaching and interacting with customers?
5. Benchmarks: how does our company or team compare?

These all bear themselves out in the data and the numbers affecting a company, and therefore need to be taken into account, when making decisions.

Altitude

Another major factor that introduces distortions and potentially causes conflict is altitude within a company. Your position affects how high up you are in the company. It is also related to what you are responsible for, and what you are interested in.

The Gamestorming guys have a practical visual which can be used to illustrate the concept:

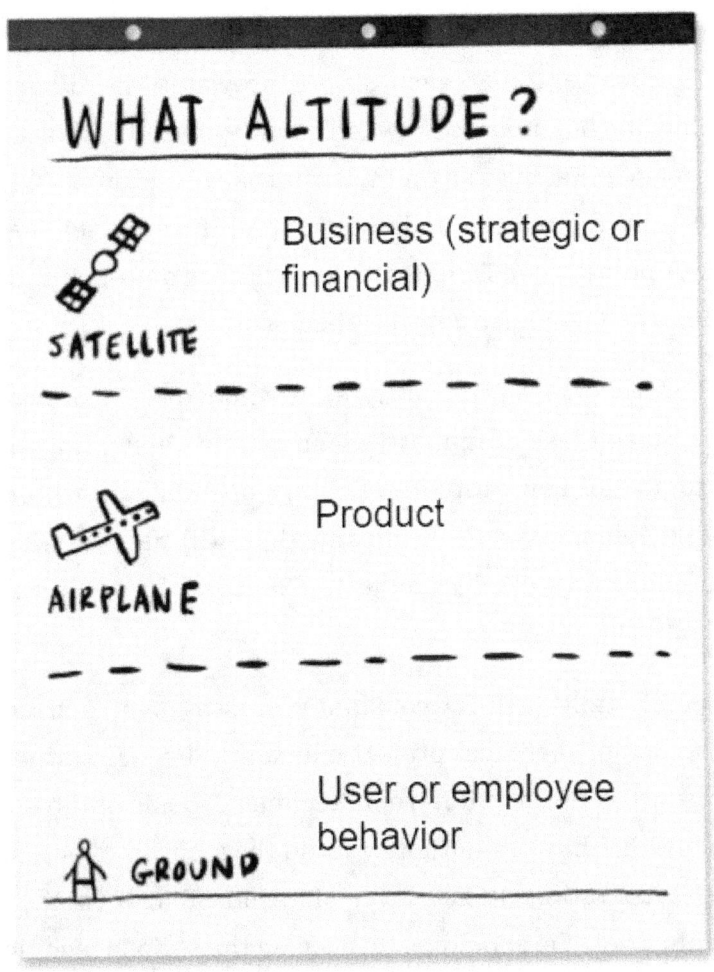

source:Gamestorming, used with permission

The concerns of the C-suite should be like a satellite. Their attention should be outside the company, on factors that would affect it significantly. In the middle, you have managers taking the strategy and insights from the satellite and flying planes, with all of the instrumentation necessary to achieve this impressive feat. Front line employees need to stay firmly grounded in serving customers, operating effectively, or the technical details of what needs to be built.

It's important that each side appreciates the other to allow for boundaries between each layer and connect all three perspectives so that it is internally consistent.[38] You each have the same understanding of the situation, each data point is consistent with every other data point, and there are no major gaps or blind spots.

The level of task granularity, as mentioned in the previous section on task granularity when defining done, is a good example of how altitude matters. Depending on where a stakeholder is in the company, they will naturally have a different level of granularity needed to be effective in their role.

For example, a CTO constantly crosses over and acts as a junior technical project manager. She shifts around resources to serve different "technical" goals of the company. She has the authority to do that, but in effect, she isn't operating at her level of responsibility. At the C-suite level, she should be focused on the serious technical challenges affecting the entire business, how to create an environment where technical staff can make the most of

---

[38] To use geeky technical jargon, you aim for "referential integrity" like in a database.

their abilities, and possibly looking at strategic opportunities and long-term trends for the company given the current technology in the company. The latter is particularly true, since market demand tends to jump quickly from one approach to another. Compare how long it took the world to adopt the use of telephones against how quickly the iPhone style of cell phone overtook Blackberries and other predecessors.

Typically, silos form in companies because there isn't enough awareness or appreciation of altitude.

Remote culture

Finally, the company's actual culture is a critical context. When everyone was working from home, company culture, i.e. how things were actually done in a company, was exposed in a low-context environment like email and chat. If managers are rewarded for toxic behavior like bullying, guilt, or building a power base through hiding details, then going remote context magnifies how employees feel about this.

In practical terms, company context is what changes when you change between remote jobs. This factor underlies the "Great Resignation" of 2021. Companies were terrified of employees leaving or burning out. While you physically sit at the same computer when changing jobs, your personal and work-from-home context remain the same, but your job context changes dramatically. If your work context causes you to burn out like corporate refugee turned career coach Jules Turner.[39], then healing the culture is the only sensible way forward that could improve the situation, not team building events like a remote, "HR-friendly" game of Cards against Humanity over scones and tea.

How to use context

Armed with this insight about the importance of context interacting with individual traits, ask! Find out about their context or if there are any significant changes. Let it become a topic of discussion, especially if you have people working from home and not sharing the office context with you simultaneously. Try to figure out each person's IF-THEN combinations as you get to know them better.

In the low context of working online: communicate frequently. Give context when you can, following the suggestions around async work from the meetings section. Share your context so that others can understand where you are "coming from".

In practice, it's important to consider each meeting participant's context, why it impacts the meeting outcome, and the overall consequences. If you are surprised, don't make assumptions, and follow up individually and validate them together in private.

---

[39] https://recommendedbyluke.com/TurnerBurnout

Key takeaways

- Working remotely is a low-context cultural experience. Act accordingly. Don't assume. Over-communicate, using the information architecture at your disposal.
- Individual traits explain behavior only when understood in context, so make sure you understand a person's context.
- Types of context worth considering: work mode vs. home mode, individual preferences, company-specific culture, including how you work remotely at that company.

Why department boundaries matter most

Contrary to popular belief, before the pandemic, most managers felt they had clear objectives and felt aligned with their immediate managers, according to HBR [40]. But there remains a massive gap between strategy and execution in many companies. According to the same article, when digging a little deeper, you discover that alignment usually only exists on an intra-team level.

The biggest challenges middle managers face when executing their company's strategy include failure to coordinate across units and failure to align. Managers also say they are 'three times more likely to miss performance commitments because of insufficient support from other units than because their own teams fail to deliver. These fault lines are critical factors in overall company performance.

In most companies, that boundary lies across functional lines. And it's usually based on budgeting authority, in the hope of being efficient at a functional department level. Having highly efficient department fiefdoms, each of which isn't aligned with other departments, won't lead to the most desired overall outcomes of high performance

---

[40] https://recommendedbyluke.com/StrategyExecutionHBR

at a company level. Even at this level, companies struggle with a whole being less valuable than the sum of its parts.

Workflow

Workflow is typically organized by functions, with long waits between each step. Efficiency within a function is meaningless to customers.

I've certainly experienced that in larger companies, where most of my time wasn't spent with the team or even senior stakeholders; it was dealing with other teams like IT and security, which weren't aligned with mine. And this is often taken for granted. Everyone assumes that this is how it must be.

Why silos are the single biggest natural barrier to alignment

Silos arise inadvertently because of historical default behavior, especially in the absence of leadership. This is on top of the "Swiss-cheese organizations" we have because people come and go frequently. If we aren't deliberate about designing company culture, choosing values, and reinforcing them, some type of culture will arise. Humans naturally create informal hierarchies and networks, regardless of whether an official one exists.

Over time, it becomes clear "how things work here":

- Who gets promoted and why.
- Who gets fired.
- Who gets the most engaging assignments.

If there isn't a cross-cutting one, each workgroup will create its own culture. It requires a leader to have a vision and reinforce values that everyone buys into.

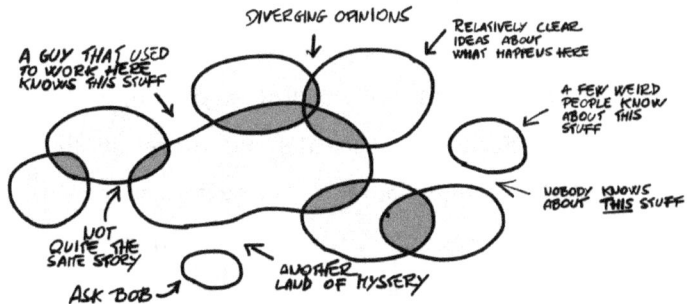

Source: *Eventstorming* by Alberto Brandolini, used with permission

In addition to naturally clumping together in little intra-company silos, the above shows what happens in an established company by default. We face a combination of:

- Information that is lost, badly explained, documented, or generally avoided unless necessary.
- The people who knew the information have often left the company; it's awkward to ask them anything, not to mention, by the time you have a precise question they don't remember the details at that level.
- There are many areas of disagreement, where the answer to a question depends on who you ask.
- People have selective memories. They might overlook details, and even if they do, they are likely to forget them over time.
- If individuals do stay at the company, often they've changed roles and don't feel responsible anymore for that particular area.

In theory, senior management has this responsibility, but often management itself can drift into becoming a silo:

"It isn't always helpful to look to the person with the most experience. Instead, look to the person with the best vantage point. Who is standing right at the juncture where things are happening? Who has the fifty-yard-line seat on the action? That person isn't always the designated leader," says Susan Scott in *Fierce Conversations*. In practice, it's enough for senior management to create the right context and delegate the responsibility closer to the action, especially for tactical "how-to" issues. This approach results in more informed decisions. From a shared perspective, you gather the same facts, making it possible to discuss and agree on the best way forward.

The silo megaphone effect

The biggest challenge I've had with building alignment as a team leader was the *"silo megaphone effect"*. Each department manager has certain objectives and assumptions reinforced by discussions with the people he's managing. They start to repeat assumptions as if they were mantras. And begin to share unique beliefs among their clique, which the rest of the organization might not agree with or support.

This can result in somewhat surreal coordination efforts across department lines. Each manager argues what is best for their particular area or metric they own. Their knee-jerk focus is on local maximization without necessarily clarifying the globally optimal outcome. This happens despite everyone having the best of intentions. I've fallen into the trap myself of arguing for a short-term benefit that will bring in the schedule at the expense of adequately solving a problem at an organizational level. Sometimes the schedule pressure was just too strong.

I've attended several surreal meetings where heads of different departments would convene to align on the topic of the moment. During the discussion, each one made statements. Out of context, each statement made absolute sense. For example, the QA person argued for keeping a certain standard in terms of quality. The delivery person wanted to bring in the date as much as possible. The product person wanted to throw in as much scope as possible to make it easier to sell the product. I understood why they were saying what each of them said. They genuinely believed they were arguing for the company's overall benefit as a whole because their experience of the company.

Nevertheless, if you juxtapose what one manager was saying against another, the statements were contradictory. It was less than clear what the overall priority was. And this is a dangerous lack of alignment.

Key takeaways

- Usually, teams are internally aligned; the bigger challenges usually lie across department lines.

How to align or realign within a company

I've done this so many times, largely intuitively, I've lost count. Yet, after a bit of stepping back, I realized that the successful attempts to align a wider team by reducing ambiguity shared the following steps:

1. Expand context deliberately
2. Prioritize the options
3. Start with the most urgent

Regardless of the starting point, these three steps will help you clarify and address the real-time needs of the organization. And it frees you from many current constraints imposed on the company, to serve the customer and all stakeholders better.

1. Expand context deliberately

In short, you are trying to get outside of the organization's current filters to share more or different information. Once you do this widely enough, the company as a whole can prioritize more effectively.

Within a company, shared meaning arises among distinct groups. This is due to perspective. While they are helpful in terms of creating focus, difficulties arise when perspectives become too narrow–especially if there is a lot of ambiguity and competition for attention. When this works, you achieve that fundamental Aristotelian goal of a whole being greater than the sum of its parts. This can occur at multiple overlapping levels:

- Individual contributor: stuck focusing on the negative aspects of a situation, making it difficult to forgive and accept in order to move on and achieve more vs. just naturally adapting to everything as it comes up
- Workgroup: team dynamic that enables high performance vs. pulls it back
- Department or division: supporting and enabling one another without piling on red tape due to fears of reoccurring past mishaps
- Division or even daughter companies: conglomerates, diversified investment funds, and focused large businesses

In my experience, the simple act of widening the perspective and focusing on the **present** often triggers realizations that help. It surfaces obvious and specific actions that need to be taken. The simple act of widening everyone's context makes it obvious where the conflicts are and what needs to be resolved. Essentially, unseen factors emerge. Often, there are several "no-brainer" moments for everyone involved once they see that wider context. That is the reaction that you're hoping for.

circle? square? or if we step back we realize it's a cylinder.

You build alignment and motivation by deliberately expanding each participant's currently perceived context. It is the single most valuable task you can do. Our goal is to smash together two or more contexts deliberately. Exposing organizational blind spots will likely produce an improved outcome, more robust than the current state. Create an opportunity for relative strangers within the company to talk. For example, embolden a timid front-line employee to share a crucial detail with a senior decision maker.

In practical terms, it's best to start with sensemaking and problem setting at the individual level, and then work up to each wider level. Start holding 1-to-1 meetings with direct reports. Find out what they are excited about, and conversely what's holding them back. Ask detailed questions around organizational blockers or enablers. If they feel safe and they trust you, you'll get a detailed picture of what needs to be fixed. If they don't, work on establishing a better personal relationship or connection with that person. And most importantly, act on it. There is nothing more disheartening than collecting honest feedback and then ignoring it. Remove blockers. Get resources. Make it happen.

Once you have a solid hub-and-spoke relationship with each person on your team, start working on team dynamics in greater depth. Be open to feedback. Help the team hold honest retrospectives around what's working and what needs improvement. At this point, you can always fall back on the individual relationship you have with each person if necessary. At this stage, you're aiming to move from a hub-and-spoke setup, to a well-integrated team that holds itself accountable.

Beyond that level, you start moving into inter-departmental or functional territory. Ensure you have executive air cover first, as many improvements in this area will result from improved policies or changed budgets. Keep coming back to customer needs and expectations–as all departments are equally accountable for whether the customer is happy. As mentioned earlier, this is usually where strategy is mapped to execution; often, this is where alignment becomes an issue. Use your skills in problem framing and clarifying priorities to help coordinate efforts across multiple departments.

The details of exactly how a situation needs to improve already lie in the details of that specific organization. But no one has the full picture. In short, there are missing conversations. You want to create a space for them to happen. You need to get into relevant enough detail to motivate change. While it's human nature to want a silver bullet that makes a problem go away by just paying enough money, when you are dealing with groups of people, it's unlikely to work that way—especially given a large enough group. People are fascinating and unpredictable.

2. Wider context enables re-prioritization

Once you discover a wider context together, you can discuss priorities for the organization with the wider audience at that meeting.

Part of the challenge of running a larger company is that larger organizations create increasing levels of abstraction for senior leadership. When you get into a stressful situation requiring change, there is a lot of information lost at each level and among the Aristotelian parts, making it even harder to align around what needs to be changed.

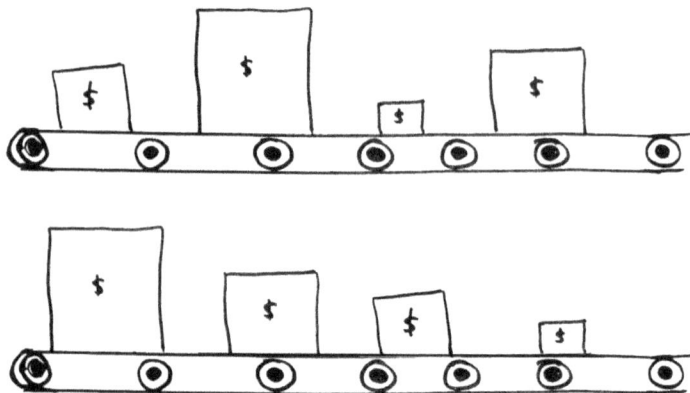

Order matters: when you do something affects its value

This enables the company to maximize value through re-ordering and splitting up work. Don Reinertsen articulates this most clearly in a product development context, in his book *The Principles of Product Development Flow*:

> "The cost of a queue is not just determined by its size; it depends on which items are delayed, and how long they are delayed. By changing the sequence in which we service the jobs in the queue, we can significantly reduce the cost of the queue."

Reinertsen encourages estimating the financial cost of delay for individual tasks, products or product features in product development. By putting financial values on delay (or timing of work), you ground the discussion in the financial implications of each option. This makes it somewhat more concrete.

The same principle applies to any non-routine work (i.e. most office work). For example, you improve a process once, but this effort benefits the company for a long time. It's highly creative and analytical. Where do you start? What can you streamline? Paying attention to the order in which you deliver work affects how much value you generate. It benefits everyone if you can eliminate mindless busywork through a streamlined process. This is true for most knowledge work.

Once a wider picture emerges, it's much easier to discuss and prioritize. It will clarify which items the company must obviously do first. For example, someone is internally blocked or prevented from achieving the "top priority" goal. By expanding decision-maker awareness, one of two positive resolutions become possible:

1. Either the goal or need isn't as important as originally thought, and something else is more important, or
2. Other things should be de-prioritized to help resolve it.

In short, this wider context enables you to **prioritize in the moment more accurately.** So while widening the context might seem to be a waste of time at first, in fact, nothing could be further from the truth. Prioritizing well in the moment based on currently known facts beats most other recipes for operating at maximum efficiency as an organization.

There are many factors to take into consideration, including:

- How many clients will care and how it impacts their experience
- The penalty for not doing something, i.e., defaulting to the present
- Risks
- Costs
- Returns
- Customer experience

You are trying to root out inconsistencies among the organizational priorities down to the workgroup or even individual level.

A game that mirrors achieving alignment at work

It's like an elaborate game of organizational Mikado: only pull on a stick if you expect it won't move or affect any other stick. If you sort out internal conflicts and dependencies now, you unblock the company to "become effortlessly" in the future.

> Here's how Mikado looks:
>
> 1. You spill out several colored sticks onto a flat surface.
> 2. Then, you take turns trying to pick out one stick at a time, without moving any of the other sticks.
> 3. If you pull out a stick successfully, you get to keep it.
> 4. At the end of the game, you tally up points based on the colors on the stick or shapes of the stick endings.
>
> Simple.
>
> But definitely difficult–(even when sober).
>
> Because it takes a lot of concentration, motor skills, and prioritization.

Mikado's a lot like managing a portfolio of projects. Especially if there are lots of projects going on at the same time. It's analogous to jumbled sticks lying on the table. The more projects you have on-at the same time-the more likely you are to experience *project deadlock*: one or more sticks blocking another from being picked up, where you need to reallocate resources from one project to another first. Which often keeps the second from ever happening or forces you to wait. As well as the twenty other projects.

Interdependencies in the pile of sticks dictate the optimal approach. It's not enough to identify the highest value stick and pull it out because of the potential dependencies. For example, let's say the requirement to not move the other sticks didn't exist (i.e., unlimited resources). If you knew that a stick with 5 colors gives you the most points, you would just pick that one up first without consequence.

But resource constraints exist. Like the other sticks which you don't want to disturb, you don't want to disrupt any projects or products. At a systemic level, you have a fixed number of people and a logical order of priorities. Surely, you could tell your team to drop everything and execute only the top priority item if that generates the most value?

The cat herding gig was easier than this...

If there are different people responsible for each project, this is even more complicated. Orchestrating this complexity becomes an art—like conducting a cat orchestra. Each project manager is out to push for their project, unaware of the overall picture or priorities. Because they want to achieve and show results in their area, but they don't realize (or prefer to ignore) the fact that the overall system they operate in determines their results. And its constraints.

And often, it's difficult to judge priorities with a lot of projects, when you're deep into the details of shifting resources between project A and project R. Because lots of projects become priorities when Scott becomes available. Or Jane from testing. So the risk is that "what customers want" becomes constrained by how quickly you can allocate resources to their pet projects, not based on what they need. Customers get what they get based on **your company's delivery constraints**.

And without transparent discussion about actual top priorities, juggling resources across a portfolio becomes like a game of Mikado. Pull off a few projects at a time, hurting none of the other ones (which by necessity levitates in space, starved of resources), just to keep up.

Another really important discussion to have is around company level priorities and projects. The more you have on in parallel, the longer you will wait for any of them to complete. If things are taking too long, are there any projects you can cancel or pause, to free up resources for the newly discovered priorities?

Start by expanding perspectives. You uncover dependencies as early as possible to ensure that they don't constrain you. There is no point in insisting on having so many "sticks" in the game if they prevent your company from achieving what matters most. This approach also helps you question starting something new, as it will be yet another potential blocker for existing priorities.

3. One step past the "No-brainers"

The trap of "fire-fighting" happens when everyone constantly focuses on urgent issues only, which usually causes problems. Heroes jump from one drama to another. But the pattern can't change until you have enough context to re-prioritize. When you have an overall picture and a sense of what is most important, you can make space for newly important work and set deadlines. At the same time, it's easier to differentiate between work that is simply called urgent or has artificially inflated urgency (e.g. setting deadlines on low priority projects), and truly urgent work. With this wider perspective and priorities, you can break unhealthy company patterns around urgency.

This is most visible in what happens directly after all fires are put out. Usually, a handful of work items are "no-brainers" from a customer and company perspective. The question is whether you have the space to execute on them or not. With many interlocking projects competing for scarce resources, like in the Mikado analogy above, typically, you struggle.

Given a large enough list of tasks, there will nearly always be at least a handful, which you must do immediately. It's almost like a law of nature. The levels of urgency around what needs to be done will vary. So having a complete list is the initial focus. That's a good basis for confirming or changing overall priorities.

- If there is a genuine crisis of any sort, with the

benefit of wider context, you will be sure that you aren't missing something even more important.
- As you discuss that list, look for all no-brainers. For example, it's just a no-brainer that you need IT to order servers ASAP. If you need a special sandbox environment for the team, one which mirrors production, the earlier you chase it down, the better.
- Often for managers, anything that blocks for something else is in that category, given the complicated nature of coordinating so many interdependencies. The sooner you unblock everyone, the sooner you'll benefit from higher team productivity.

Those will keep you busy as a leader for some time. Once you resolve the no-brainers, you will have time to revisit your priorities and start working on those. With fires put out and no-brainers addressed, you'll find it increasingly easier to continue prioritizing because now you've started preventing future "fires".

Companies often let low priority work creep in and push out the effort needed to address the root causes of serious and urgent problems. Make sure you make an effort to solve the immediate problem, and also take any steps you can to prevent it from happening again. When done, then you move on to the next priority. If you do that consistently, the number of urgent crises goes down.

In short, having a prioritized list of urgent and important tasks as a group is the starting point for talking about allocation, responsibility, and getting to "done". The challenge lies in conflicts among different subgroups: globally as a company, departments, teams, and so on. As long as you use the customer or a top market segment as the final arbiter of priorities, eventually you will reduce ambiguity enough that the pressure and interruptions die down.

Core techniques to trigger sensemaking

Two primary areas where you want to expose ambiguity are the company's understanding of customers, and its understanding of its own processes. Ideally, the best approach is visual and collaborative, so that everyone converges on the same perspective. Follow this kind of exercise with interviews of the affected parties, especially customers.

Customer profiling

Once there is more established interest in doing something practical, it's worth holding a group customer profiling exercise. Customers have a uniquely global view of your organization and its products or services. As mentioned earlier, customers don't care about your efforts; they only care about what your company can do for them.

A customer persona helps ground any change efforts in what customers find valuable. You can use any persona tool, like the Hero Canvas[41] for example, to map out

---
[41] https://recommendedbyluke.com/HeroCanvas

assumptions about who customers and prospects are and what they care about.

The power of customer profiling, combined with customer interviews, is enormous. At one client site, the potential service features for a new initiative went from 27 down to 1, with 2 other features as a possibility for a few cases. Everything else sounded nice within the company's "echo chamber" of assumptions about what customers want but would have been a colossal waste of resources.

Visual process mapping

It can also be helpful to map out customers', markets, or internal processes. Using post-its to visualize events, steps, or sequences helps you see how the action unfolds over time. Breaking down complicated domains visually means that anyone can take part, despite their background and skill set, i.e. it can include a mix of technical and non-technical staff.

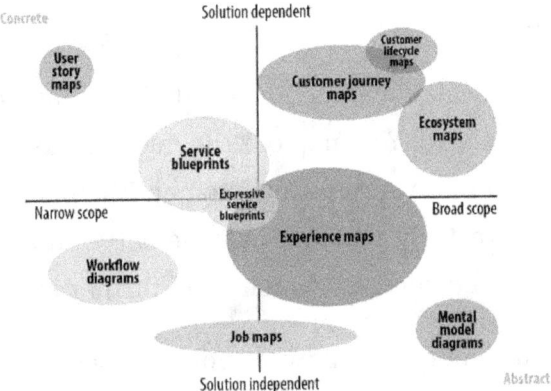

Map types available to explore ambiguity, source: James Kalbach, used with permission

The three most useful types of maps are:

- Customer experience maps: how a customer interacts at multiple touchpoints with your company, to identify what that experience is actually like
- Workflow diagrams or maps: if it's not customer facing, but nonetheless problematic it can be extremely useful to map out workflows–especially if they span multiple departments
- Customer journeys: unlike a customer experience map, this focuses primarily on the path from the customer being unaware of the company's solution to becoming a fully-fledged customer

For in-depth descriptions of the above as well as other options, check out *Experience Mapping* by James Kalbach. If your company struggles with internal bottlenecks, a visual approach helps everyone step outside of their immediate local view. Mapping out "how things work" with several stakeholders across departments brings everyone together.

This is a special application of the mapping exercise mentioned above. You map out the micro-tasks and steps that happen when serving a customer. It helps you define problems precisely, which is half the battle. It also identifies unresolved conflicts which need further attention.

When you're done, apply what you've discovered to day-to-day operations. How can you change the daily workflow to take advantage of your insights? Do an open brainstorm around this. Then agree how specific individuals will implement these ideas (and agree on deadlines!).

If there are too many, prioritize them. Only do a handful. Implement them in the order of expected impact.

Summary

In building alignment for the long term, we redesign the organizational context through effective conversations. The social infrastructure changes when conversations occur around what matters. This redesign solves the immediate problem; but it also helps prevent sliding back into the same defaults in the future. Once established, the newly deepened relationships reinforce the improved context.

After aligning successfully, you may eventually have another crisis of some type. This will require you to cycle through the same process. Often, this will happen with similar participants, although you should try to question if any important stakeholders are missing. This enables a wider yet more granular view of current problem areas.

This leads us to the next important question of who needs to be involved in order to make this happen. In the next chapter, we'll start with departments, as that is a common problem area.

Key takeaways

- If left to their own devices, large organizations will naturally drift into silo-ed disarray.
- Use crises as opportunities to align across the company. If necessary, redesign the organization for an improved flow of work.
- Many conflicts arise in companies because each side pays attention to or notices different facts without the benefit of full context.
- There are 3 steps to achieving alignment:
    1. Expand context
    2. Prioritize
    3. Look one step past the no-brainers

If the direct approach fails

In a context with multiple conflicts and disconnects at play, the wisest starting point is to find common ground. If a team is not aligned, they don't agree on what's important. So that's pretty much the beginning of everything else.

While this may seem somewhat indirect, it's a critical part of creating an environment where you can negotiate through the differences across groups. I call it "right angle consensus building".

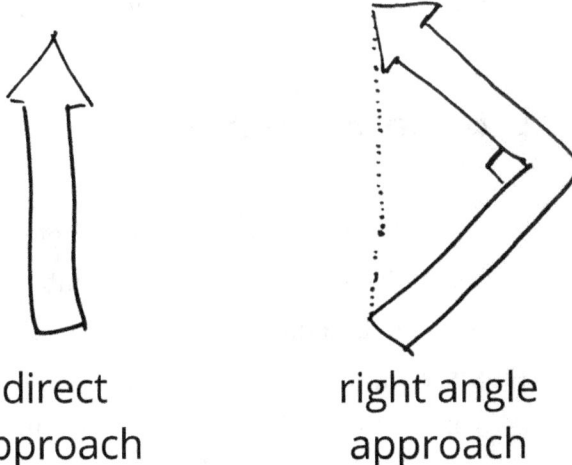

If the direct approach fails, try right angles.

As a starting point, the direct way is often first, especially if you think there is already enough psychological safety to speak your mind. If they feel safe, team members will express their concerns. Going the direct, or "straight line" route may not be the most effective way, especially if there is a difficult atmosphere around a team or a product. People can lock up if they feel unduly confronted. And they won't feel safe enough to give negative feedback.

In this case, you need to take a right-angle approach.

First, establish the cross-cutting common ground among the whole group, before you start building upwards. In particular, focus on the absolute baseline of what holds the group together: a shared value. If the group is going through a difficult patch, it's likely that this value isn't being articulated or, more importantly, lived by the group. A virtue, not just a declared value. Instead of just presuming anything, align the group explicitly around this virtue, earn the team's trust, and figure out what's next.

How this works in practice

In *The Power of Habit*, Charles Duhigg recounts a fabulous story about Alcoa, the aluminum manufacturer and the late Paul O'Neil, their now legendary CEO. When Paul joined the company, Alcoa was in a significant crisis. They were losing money left and right. Lots of uncertainty about the company's future. The unions were unhappy because employees were unnecessarily getting significantly injured or dying.

Paul's background was mostly in government as a civil servant. He had a long career creating unexpectedly positive change when serving in the US State Department.

In his inaugural Alcoa CEO meeting with Wall Street equity research analysts, Paul gets up on the stage. They expected him to talk about things like EBITDA (earnings before interest, taxes, depreciation, and amortization). Instead, he effectively said, "I want to talk to you today about employee safety". His primary concern was improving processes so that union workers would be safe. And presumably, this was based on his legwork. He spoke with everyone he could in the company. Given the message, it was pretty clear he got outside of the executive suite offices. He spoke with people on the smelting floor. He spoke with middle managers. Those conversations showed that everyone cared about safety, even if they were not necessarily willing to name it publicly.

People were getting hurt or dying while at work. That was his primary concern. It went against his values and the values of the individuals at the company, but the company wasn't doing anything to stop it.

Clearly, the factory workers had a vested interest in a safe working environment, particularly since it was unsafe. Going up management lines and losing workers had business impacts, in addition to the tragic loss of a person. It also meant productivity dropped along with morale. Even after recruiting a replacement, they wouldn't necessarily see an improvement.

The effects reverberated across the rest of the company.

Beyond just the line manager's view, accidents were a PR disaster. And one PR disaster followed another, which impacted recruitment and marketing. At the executive board level, this was showing up as continuously increasing losses when monitoring finances. It might not have been evident that the human tragedy of losing people was the root cause of their financial troubles. At least, looking at it from a textbook accounting perspective.

Using "safety" as a guiding principle in their decision making required having the courage to commit to:

1. One priority
2. That specific priority
3. A shared lens to evaluate every other decision

In effect, this made everyone focus on that one thing.

The value here is worker safety which was completely in line with what everyone actually valued. Therefore, everyone could come together and use that as a lens through which to make decisions. When considering options around a decision, the first question is how each option will influence employee safety. This is the key criterion. This is true for the decision itself, when a decision needs to be made, and what the implications are for various groups within the company.

As soon as Paul O'Neill started repeating the safety mantra over and over, he faced incredulity. This fancy know-it-all CEO who's come in from outside of the industry is telling us how to run our day-to-day. Not without reason, the factory workers suspected his true motives were hidden. It wasn't until there were a couple of difficult situations and conflicts, where the company had to start publicly making decisions. And clearly Paul O'Neill stood behind the choices leading to greater workplace safety, prioritizing that over other options even if they were easier, quicker, or cheaper. The front line started to believe that their safety matters to the company at all levels.

At that point, the company's fortunes started turning around. Accident rates dropped. The effectiveness of the existing teams increased. Overall morale went up. The morale improvement trickled up to the entire company. Ultimately, there was a pretty clear positive financial impact, where operating costs went down. To some extent, knowing that everyone comes to work happy is its own reward. They're working with people that they enjoy working with, they enjoy their work, and they're engaged.

How I applied this in software

When I came across this story, I was fired up to find an analogous value for my teams. Clearly, physical safety wasn't as big of a concern in an office environment. I had to isolate the characteristics of that solution to transplant it into my own context.

The three primary groups, at least within the team that I had to deal with, were business analysts (BA), the developers, and quality assurance (QA) people. The developers were quite keen on playing with new technologies and the intellectual challenge of figuring out how to solve problems while building tech. The QA people enjoyed trying to break things to figure out where there were any weak points, and they signed off on whether a piece of work was completed. The business guys were keen on achieving a certain business result and mapping that to customer needs. Specific features addressed those needs. So I started from the ground up: having many one-on-one discussions with team members to ask about how to organize the team's work.

At the time, I had inherited a dispirited team who were nudged into completing a bunch of code quickly. While the team went along with it, they had been asked to rush the coding part to make it look like they were "dev done" as quickly as possible. In that state, though, the code was un-releasable anyway. So it was essentially more of an internal win that had no customer impact. As the developers were furiously coding, QA was bored because there was little to do. Then, once the code existed, developers were bored with fixing a very high volume of bugs. And this was dragging on for months, without any true ability to estimate when it would all end.

I realized that the "common ground" across these three groups was that they all wanted to produce a high-quality product. Each had slightly different definitions of what quality meant, but these were essentially just functional perspectives. There could be various approaches to achieving high quality. It was pretty much a case of working back from that end goal, all the way through to define a day-to-day process that resulted in slices of high quality product, one feature at a time. We workshopped it. The group defined a standard that we wanted to work towards. And designed a process, so that anything produced would be of high quality. We were willing to trade scope for quality. In other words, it was better to ship fewer features, but deliver them at high quality.

A key component here was feedback. To be precise: multiple interim feedback loops. Ideally, any piece of work would aim for high quality at all times. QA was supposed to get only products that the other teams were happy with. By the time a piece of software even gets to QA, it's already been through rigorous specification by the business analysts and automated testing by the developers themselves. QA had a high bar for quality by definition. We were at least aiming to produce something that we were proud of as a team.

At least, in theory. QA's biggest struggles in this approach were around the quality and thoroughness of the specifications. While the software worked as the BAs and developers agreed, all the details related to expected functionality didn't reach the documentation. By the time QA got to it, they often had clarifying questions. This revealed weaknesses in the process, so we tried tightening and automating the work to minimize errors via even more automated checking. By the time we said something was done, it was high quality work. By emphasizing craftsmanship and quality, the business analysts and the developers also wanted to apply a high bar, in terms of finishing product. This team connected with the value behind the standard and embedded it into the delivery process. From my perspective, they looked more motivated as the process tapped into a deeper value of craftsmanship.

And more importantly, quality became our team's equivalent of Alcoa's workplace safety: turning quality into a prioritization lens. We looked at pretty much everything in terms of its impact on quality. Quality pulled together developers and QA into one unit, instead of squabbling fiefdoms, which was how they were used to working. And I kept reporting back to the team how our team's output and completion rate of completely finished features looked.

With such deliberate awareness around quality, it helped draw attention to good and bad habits that affected the code's resulting quality. We shared any good habits across the entire team. We looked to replace bad habits and brainstormed alternative approaches. In a workshop, we drilled down from quality as an abstract concept to specific steps or actions which could be taken when completing a specific feature or task. We essentially coached each other to help figure out the best possible way to aim for quality, while still being pragmatic.

From the point of view of having the team working well, we did achieve it. It's important to note that this was a type of work where everyone was assigned full time to this effort. And also there was a lot of overlap across what each person did, so they could jump in and help out if needed.

I think what's important here isn't so much the fact

that we aligned around quality. There was one value that was common to everyone. We discovered it through exploratory discussions within the team. Once this became clear, I agreed with executives and sponsors on the team's behalf by elaborating on the impact on the delivery schedule. And on an operational level, all of our discussions were around achieving better quality by applying the standard we decided. Or clarifying and improving it as needed. Turning this abstract & wooly concept into healthy team execution habits and rituals became the essence of how it ultimately made a difference for us.

The only thing that I was focused on was high-quality team output. Quality was an explicit step. When we said that something was completed, it already had been formally tested. We only gave the team credit for finishing the work when it was through quality. To speed up the overall pace of work, we had to optimize for completing that last step by only submitting high-quality work for testing. After some brainstorming, the developers suggested writing automated tests. So before they would even give a feature to the QA team, they would also write tests that cross-checked the requirements automatically, similar to how double-entry bookkeeping helps prevent accounting errors. As a result, they caught many bugs in their work before it even got to QA. So even though the quality was a step, we optimized the entire flow to check quality continuously. Over time, there were fewer and fewer problems right before completing the task.

In practice, adhering to our right-angle virtue of quality was a daily struggle. It was definitely a good ideal to aim for. And sometimes, we had to speed up development for internal demo purposes, but it cost us in terms of quality. We'd spend much more time making up the difference. Paradoxically, quality first was faster for our team, as an approach from the beginning. Even though it seems like it's more work, developers have to write extra tests and take on extra work, but you don't have any bugs later. Suddenly, you are much better at estimating when you'll be done and how much work is left because you can assume there will be very few bugs, thus eliminating delays. Slippage disappears. And that makes senior decision-makers very happy.

From a high level, the high focus on quality meant that we only produced work we were happy with. At a strategic level, quality was expressed as a product level tradeoff. A common pattern in enterprise software is that quality is an afterthought, or you identify bugs you can live with, but you get the bloated and buggy software out the door. In contrast, we would rather produce fewer items of higher individual value or priority yet be certain that they were high quality. Because we explicitly articulated it this way, it was clear that this was actually a virtue and not just a value. A virtue is something we were willing to give up something for and to clarify how we want to live according to the virtue. Once we were explicit about it being a value, we turned it into a virtue by operationalizing it and building it into the team's process.

How to identify your company's right-angle virtue

Edward Deming, the famed statistician, observed that "94% of problems are due to common causes and are management's responsibility." This statistic refers to the context and working conditions in which work happens. Issues are typically systemic. Often only symptoms are noticed, but little happens beyond that. Instead, most executives focus on problems with individual employees or staffing teams. Yet according to how Deming defined it, only 6% of problems at the companies he studied are due to special causes, which included problems with individual employees. By taking ownership of employee context as a leader, you unleash employees' ability to contribute. And you focus on improving productivity by enabling people to give more rather than trying to extract more from them.

Every time I discovered a right-angle virtue, it grew out of one-to-one discussions with every individual on the team about improving their work experience. Questions will ideally flow from conversations but should ideally follow along these lines:

1. How do you want to work?
2. Is there anything blocking you, especially in your environment?
3. Do you see or experience anything at work that concerns you or impacts your productivity?

4. Is there anything I can do to help you produce more or feel more productive?
5. Are there any people who can help you complete more work? Is anyone or any external team keeping you from achieving it?
6. What motivates you to work here?

I suspect it's refreshing for most employees to be asked these questions-because they do not often come up. Many contextual factors drive their productivity downward, factors which are invisible at higher altitudes in the company. Often, the line employees are painfully aware of these factors, so they are happy to provide input. If these are resolved, it builds trust in the leader who resolved it.

Look for patterns in the problems and concerns they express. There will likely be some. Also, think about unmet needs and articulate them as a value which is not being met.

After you address the most pressing issues that emerge from the discussions, you can speak with the wider team, including senior stakeholders, to share your findings from the interviews. Then figure out how to operationalize the value and turn it into a virtue using a workshop format.

Stepping back

This whole approach speaks to the very fractal nature of running distributed teams. Evolving the right approach out of simple changes is best because the final approach will produce results in your context. And if it doesn't, you need to break down what you're doing into smaller parts and keep testing. Your best tools are the ones that you evolve as a team. Your approach needs to work for your particular team, in your specific conditions, with that specific set of people, for that specific context.

It's dangerous to think in terms of best practices that you copy-paste into your organization without that contextual awareness. They may work or they may backfire. Remote effectiveness is context specific. However, if you do identify a simple thing that is working, you extrapolate from there. Keep repeating it. Tweaking it. Evolving it by adding simple changes. Over time, it will be more complex, but one that's increasingly customized for your team, your company, and your context.

This approach of identifying a value that isn't being upheld is the starting point to creating alignment. You don't want to be imposing an alignment with an externally defined strategy on a bunch of unsuspecting employees. Quite the opposite. Create space. Explore current pain points in the context of current challenges. Identify disconnects with values which people are disappointed about: the problems you're trying to solve as an organization, the difficulties you're facing, and any bottlenecks you have.

Particularly in the context of a larger organization, where you typically already have:

- Budget to hire decent people if you need them

- Many assets
- Many strengths

Quite often, your challenges relate to effective coordination of company assets and bringing them together in a way that serves your customers.

"Just let me check on Google first, and I'll be right with you."

And that's often where the gap between strategy and execution lies. In fact, you can't just hire a subject matter expert who waves a magic wand that makes all the woes go away. By definition, there are many complex-moving (often inter-dependent) parts. Figuring out how to get them to orchestrate, to work together, and ideally, to self-organize so that the customer feels served.

Key takeaways

- Alignment is highly context-specific, in particular due to the specific people involved.
- Speaking with the people involved will always be the starting point, to discovering their full context.

- Figure out what most people struggle with and identify the underserved value.
- Rally everyone around that one specific point and focus all discussion around that value.
- Help each person apply that value when working on specific problems they face.

How to break down silos in your company

At its core, the key missing element in silos is the inability to make sense of what the other parts of the company are doing. Everyone is working from different facts, assumptions, and perspectives. So the goal is to break that down as quickly as possible. If there is too much focus on execution, each "part" executes according to its own logic, and rules given from above. And that quickly leads to the conflicts mentioned above.

The best way to help break down silos permanently is to reorganize work around cross-functional teams. Here's what I mean:

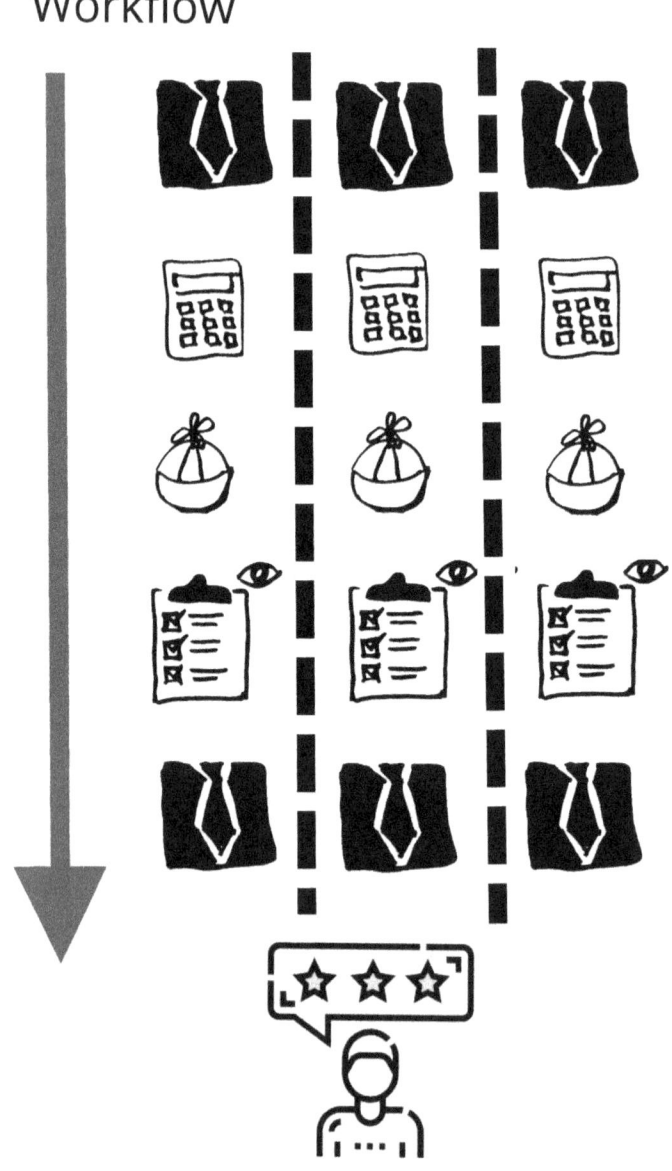

Organize work around what customers expect by prioritizing cross-functional delivery

Cross-functional teams combine various functional abilities, but each is autonomous and responsible for its own business results. In fact, cross-functional teams already exist under many guises:

- Committee
- Task force
- Project or product team
- Executive board (yep, they're a cross-functional team, too)!

The key starting point is to tie each cross-functional team with the impact on customers. Then customers get the sense that the company is serving their needs effectively. To get this right, cross-functional teams need to be appropriately nested and aligned with functional teams to get the full effect.

And the best way to identify any blind spots quickly (and relatively painlessly) is to use sense-making meetings. Elise Keith, the author of *Where the Action Is*, comments:

> Sense-making meetings are the ones where we get together, just to understand something better. Often you'll hear a company has really entrenched silo problems. Do things like run a series of fishbowls or other kinds of exercises, where they invite people from each department. Each one has an opportunity to share: "This is what we do. This is what makes us happy. This is where we run into trouble." And then folks listen and ask questions and they take turns. Then the other thing that you can do is sit

> in on the real meetings, like the day-to-day team cadence meetings. Especially, regular action reviews [or retrospectives].... Bring people together. What did you see? What did you learn? What should we do? Get together to understand something better. Fishbowls [are a good format]. Invite people from different departments to share. Folks listen and ask questions.

Case study: Zingermans

One of the most effective tools for preventing silo formation that I've heard of exists at Zingerman's. Originally a deli, they've scaled their retail business significantly to several other business units. And one of the useful and transferrable parts of that is what they call an internal training "passport". Maggie Bayless, the managing partner at ZingTrain, their training arm, explained Zingerman's approach [42] in a Forbes piece. People joining the company are given a training roadmap, and asked to take responsibility for their own training and onboarding for their first 90 days. This passport is signed off by the training leads each time a unit is completed. The training leads themselves are operators within the different parts of the business, not just trainers. Once the onboarding is complete, the employee has built-in incentives to go and continue taking more training.

---

[42] https://recommendedbyluke.com/zingermans

One of the really important details is that the employee is exposed to many of the businesses, with workshops being led by insiders in the other daughter companies. It forges connections with that person as a jumping off point should there ever be a question about that business unit in the future, in addition to sharing what is working in that business.

Employees then go to different sub-businesses and collect stamps after completing training that is both specific to that business and applicable to the business as a whole. The goal is to constantly share ideas and then bring something that works in the coffee shop business to the candy business or the deli business.

Training Plan: General ZCoB Orientation

Name:

Position:

Timeframe: By Day 60

Reward/Consequence: Complete orientation and qualify for benefits/No benefits

Knowledge Area	Tasks	Training Vehicles	Tests/Measurement	Sign-Off/ Date
ZCoB Overview	• Attends Welcome to ZCoB	• Class (2 hours)	• Passport stamped	
	• Attends Zingerman's Employment Experience	• Class (2 hours)	• Passport stamped	
	• Passes Knife Certification Test	• Class • Handout	• Written and performance test	
	• Passes Facts of ZCoB Life Test	• Handout	• Written test	
Customer Service	• Attends The Art of Giving Great Service	• Class (2 hours)	• Passport stamped	
	• Passes Basic Customer Service Test	• Handout	• Written test	
Sanitation & Safety	• Attends Food Safety Class *	• Class (2 hours)	• Passport stamped	
Finance	• Attends a department huddle that reviews a DOR board	• Huddle	• Passport stamped	
	• Passes Basic Food Safety & Sanitation 101 Test *	• Handout	• Written test	

* NOTE: You cannot work beyond 60 days unless these two requirements are completed.
* NOTE: You have 30 days from the date you complete orientation to sign up for medical insurance. If you miss this window, you must to wait until next open enrollment (March each year) to sign up.

Note that the passport is stamped when a step is completed, source:ZingTrain, used with permission

As you can see from the above table, some evaluation happens as a formal written and performance test, like a Knife Certification Test. But then other training topics require a passport stamp like the "Art of Giving Great Service." In theory, this can be given by someone from any of the retail business units.

In addition to onboarding, there is a built in system, whereby employees are expected to upskill after being at the company for a while. This, in turn, increases the amount of interaction people have with other parts of the business.

Ultimately, if and when they do come together to make bigger decisions, the meeting feels more like a family reunion than a gaggle of antagonistic stakeholders.

How to re-focus on customer needs

Often lack of alignment is due to internal power struggles, which end up isolating "internal" departments from exposure to customers and prospects. This can breed a type of complacency that is completely justified. If someone doesn't have any contact with customers, how can they be expected to act in accordance with customer needs?

At one client site, a manager told me that he feels as though he's trapped in a bureaucratic onion. While it was nice that he felt in the center of the action, in fact what mattered was the view from the outer edges of the company. And what they were seeing in the market. But he was being shut out. So even though he wanted to understand what customers needed in order to prioritize tactical development work, the stonewalling and gamesmanship kept him inside the onion. Thus, despite his role as a product manager, the existing relationships between sales staff and customers were given priority, thus making it difficult for him to connect with customers.

In this case, a good starting point is to use a customer profiling tool, like my Hero Canvas[43], for example. This helps model current assumptions about customers, in an effort to improve the customer experience. As a workshop exercise, it can help focus everyone across the company based on what they know and what they assume, and to have a productive discussion. The simple fact of focusing on an ideal customer will shift the focus externally, and should help reduce in-fighting and internal gamesmanship. It will also help produce a working definition of value. Because the customer only cares about the perceived value your company produces. And there can easily be a lot of time wasted on efficiently doing or creating something that is irrelevant to customers. This is a good starting point for many other workshopping tools to break down what can be improved together.

Key takeaways

- Cross-functional work that addresses existing or future customer needs breaks down departmental silos.

---

[43] https://recommendedbyluke.com/HeroCanvas

What you can do now

Start by creating a safe and creative space where individuals can collaborate. In his book *Right to Left*, Mike Burrows notes that **"most failures are failures of collaboration."** If all individual contributors know and agree:

1. what needs to happen,
2. who to collaborate with,
3. why they want to collaborate,

then you will prevent strife and maximize results.

There are two levels to alignment, both intimately related to motivation. At a surface level, alignment is about exchanging knowledge about what needs to be done together, why it needs to be done, and deciding how to do it. At a deeper level, alignment builds connections and relationships. Over time, alignment will help break down barriers organically among subgroups within a larger organization. You can improve alignment by acting at both levels.

Sensemaking meetings explore internal "unknown unknowns"

Organize meetings that deliberately initiate new conversations. Your goal is to increase context awareness, so that it improves prioritization at all levels without the need for manager intervention.

In particular, aim to create conversations outside the typical patterns. Often, communication in a hierarchical company flows up and down the hierarchy only, which is how silos form.

Instead, aim to help individuals on the hierarchy to explore and meet. Help them discover how their work impacts peers across the organization and how to serve customers best.

Fireside chat

For example, you can organize a "fireside chat" with an internal expert. This can either be a monologue or an interview. The expert shares a story, perspective, or angle that many employees need to hear. This doesn't require PowerPoint slides. It doesn't need to be formal. It just needs to happen where most employees feel comfortable. An expert shares a relevant personal experience, even if she isn't known as an expert in that domain. This implicitly sends the message that anyone can contribute based on their experiences.

Fireside chats can be organized as traditional synchronous meetings, but you also have alternatives. You can release a fireside chat as an internal company podcast episode. You can organize a meeting in a case study format, where:

1. The expert describes the context and problem.

2. You poll the audience for their opinions and thoughts.
3. Finally, the expert shares what actually happened.

This format contextualizes knowledge in the company. With it, you can inform teams of technical novelties. You can share stories about how employees apply company values. In short, it's a highly versatile format, and doesn't require expensive production to be effective.

Fishbowl

The fishbowl format also breaks down boundaries. Organize a fishbowl with stakeholders from multiple departments or teams. Ideally, the individual participants rarely speak to one other. But they should be open to participating in "new/innovative" efforts that involve change.

What is a fishbowl? Bart Doorenwert of peerlearning.is[44] describes it like this:

> When you're dealing with bigger groups, it prevents the chaos of everybody talking about everything at the same time. You hold an open panel discussion where you have an expert in a chair, but then you start with other free chairs. People from the room can participate. Participants go to the stage when they want to speak. They sit on the chair and join in the conversation with a rule that there is always one empty chair. One person comes from the room and sits

---
[44] https://peerlearning.is

on the empty chair. Then the agreement is that one of the [previously] sitting people should stand down and go back to their seat, leaving one open chair again. And it ensures conversation keeps flowing. Anybody who has a question or something to share about something that's relevant or happening on stage at that moment [can] just jump up and join.

This helps break down any perceived boundaries among cliques, uniting them around the "topic of interest." If you can, include an executive sponsor, who is interested in the topic and in improving motivation and alignment. This person's presence simplifies getting budget later, if you cover anything important during the meeting.

It's easy to adapt this to an online format using tools like video conferencing e.g. zoom or whiteboards e.g. Miro. [45]

Customer profiling

Once there is more established interest in doing something practical, it's worth holding customer profiling exercises. Customers have a uniquely global view of your organization and its products or services. As Helio Fred Garcia notes in *The Power of Communication*, "Audiences have their own ideas, their own concerns, their own frames of reference. And if we want to maintain their trust and confidence, we need to start by taking those ideas,

---

[45] https://recommendedbyluke.com/virtualFishbowl for fishbowls with video conferencing tool or

concerns, and frames of references seriously." As mentioned earlier, customers don't care about your efforts; they only care about what your company can do for them.

A customer persona helps you ground change efforts in what customers find valuable. For example, you can use any persona tool, like the Hero Canvas[46] to map out assumptions about who customers and prospects are, and what they care about.

Visual process mapping

It can also be helpful to map out customers, markets, or internal processes. Using post-its to visualize events, steps, or sequences helps you see how the action unfolds over time. Breaking down complicated domains visually means that anyone can take part, despite their background and skill set, i.e., it can include a mix of technical and non-technical staff.

For example, I worked with a team who was introducing a product to the music industry. Despite having some expertise, mapping out the "life of a song" from start to finish (including where it was being monetized) helped them identify gaps in their practical knowledge. It provided a skeleton for further validation and planning. Bringing together different perspectives and multiple pairs of eyes on the same thing identifies gaps in understanding. When you're finished, the participants walk away with the same shared perspective on the problem area, which may be

---

[46] https://recommendedbyluke.com/HeroCanvas

more valuable over the life of the project than any agreed immediate next steps.

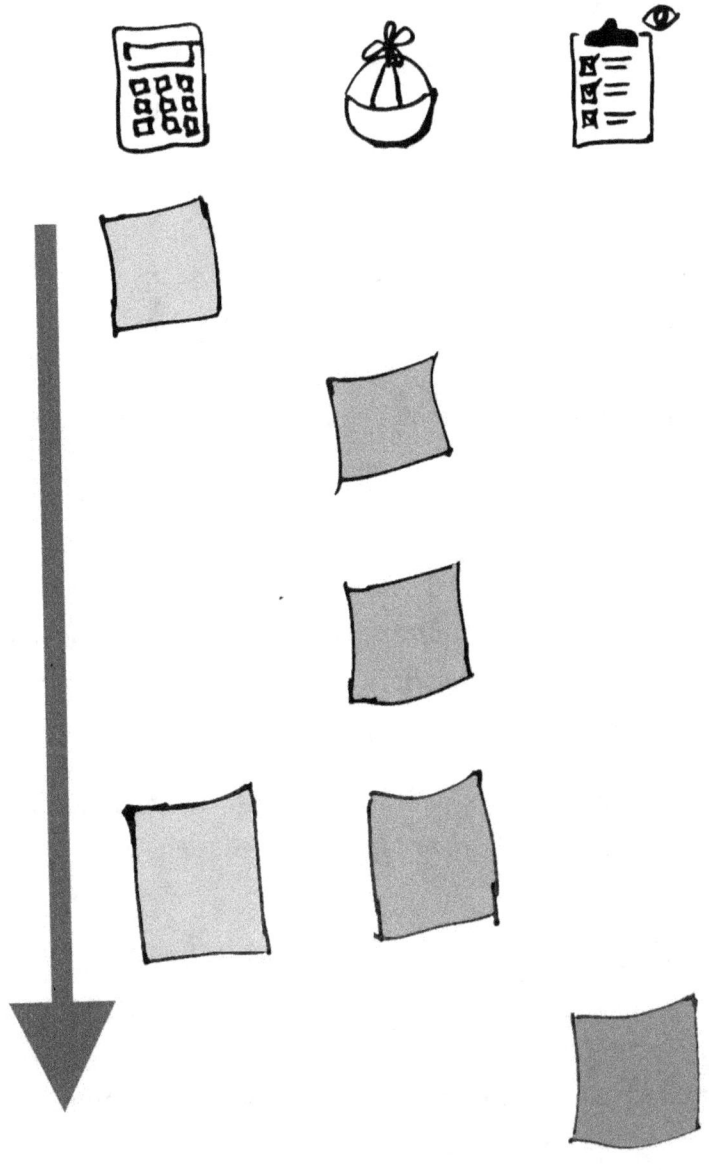

Map out interactions between functional areas

If your company struggles with internal bottlenecks, a

visual approach helps everyone step outside their immediate local view. Mapping out "how things work" with several stakeholders across departments brings everyone together.

This is a special application of the mapping exercise mentioned above. You map out the micro-tasks and steps that happen when serving a customer. It helps you define problems precisely, which is half the battle. It also identifies unresolved conflicts which need further attention.

When you're done, apply what you've discovered to day-to-day operations. How can you change the daily workflow in order to take advantage of your insights? Do an open brainstorm around this, then agree on how specific individuals will implement these ideas (and agree on deadlines!).

If there are too many, prioritize them. Only do a handful. Implement them in the order of expected impact.

Monday notes

For example, a low-tech way of systematically expanding perspective deliberately comes from NASA. Wernher von Braun [47] and his teams developed the rocket that propelled NASA's first moon mission. To encourage cross-department communication and thoughtful dissent, he asked all of his managers to submit written updates every Monday. (Granted, this was before printers were

---
[47] https://recommendedbyluke.com/MondayNotes

common in an office, much less email). When his managers submitted these, he would hand-write comments in the margin. He then photocopied his thoughts in the context of his updates, with one copy for each submitting manager. As a result, every one got feedback on their part of the company. This workflow can easily be replicated with digital tools like Google Docs or Confluence using commenting features.

The managers also gained a view of how their team's efforts fit in with the wider company as well as larger problems. "Monday Notes" made it ok to ask for help or send uncomfortable messages up the chain. Interestingly, when his successor took over and had somewhat of a short fuse, the quality of the Notes fell significantly. In short, if it helps the rocket scientists and it's pretty easy to understand, why not use it yourself in a digital-friendly way?

Retrospectives

Once you act on these insights, organize regular retrospective meetings. Tools like Retrium[48], whiteboards like Miro[49], or even free tools like Ideaboardz[50] are useful for this. These meeting types increase how much the company "senses and responds". In turn, you ensure activities are more "fit-for-purpose" when spending resources. Ultimately, retrospectives are a tool for increasing the

---
[48] https://www.retrium.com
[49] https://www.miro.com
[50] https://www.ideaboardz.com

amount of feedback a team gets. Even if it is self-generated, feedback helps improve future efforts and team self-alignment to objectives.

Cross department participation

Reassess how you can inject representatives from different departments or business lines into regular cadence meetings. It's important to "show" what's being worked on as much as possible and not rely solely on "telling" about activity. Everyone involved in a meeting will pick up different details, and it helps minimize subjective interpretation of status.

In an agile format, it's often enough to pull potential stakeholders into sprint demos. That way, they learn in context. They also don't experience a major pull on their time. Even if you aren't responsible for doing the work, having this perspective makes it much easier to set expectations and manage relationships.

Specific techniques to test

Two specific techniques that I've found helpful are the fist-to-five method of confirming alignment or understanding, as well as "disagree and commit" as a way of moving ahead quickly.

Fist to five method

The First-to-Five method [51] is a powerful technique similar to the children's game: "Rock, Paper, Scissors". When remote, you can fist-to-five on camera while videoconferencing.

Here's how it works. You are nearing the end of an important point in a group discussion. You have articulated a proposal, and you want to check how much others agree with it.

---

[51] https://recommendedbyluke.com/FistToFive

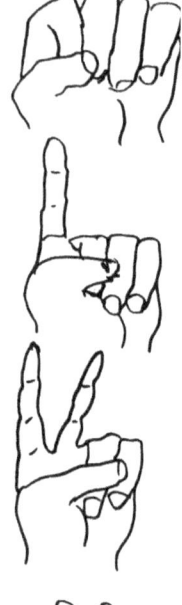

No, I object and
block the vote if I can.

I have serious reservations,
and want to resolve them.

I don't like this but
I'll go along.

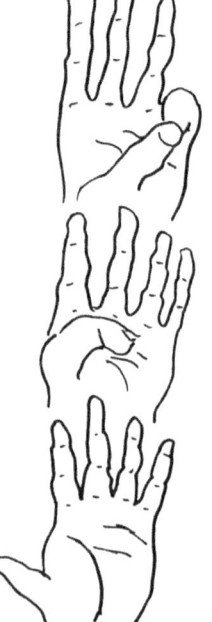

I support the idea and
like parts of it.

This idea sounds good and
maybe we can go further.

Best idea ever!!!

1. You call for a fist-to-five vote.

2. On your signal, every participant holds up zero to five fingers to show how much they agree with the proposal. Five implies complete agreement; zero stands for complete disagreement. As a variant, zero can also serve as a "veto." The fist can stop a decision completely.
3. Everyone sees the range of agreement in the group and can discuss it. If there is still a wide range of disagreement, ask someone who strongly disagrees to explain why. And follow this with one opinion of someone who strongly agrees with the proposal. This contrast brings out a fuller picture of the proposal, as well as supporting details.
4. Repeat step 3 as necessary and continue the discussion until you: achieve alignment, decide it's not important to agree now and/or, agree on threshold conditions, so that you know when to revisit the decision.
5. After this process ends, allow the actual decision makers to make the call.

Because fist-to-five is quick to do and technologically independent, it can provide value in real-time. The numbers themselves aren't as important as the discussion around the issues after seeing each participant's fingers.

It also helps reduce bias, which improves decision quality. For example, fist-to-five makes it safe to voice disagreement, if needed. It reduces biases like defaulting to the highest paid person's opinion (HiPPO), even though this person might not have full context. Fist-to-five helps reduce groupthink, i.e., when participants don't raise legitimate objections in order to maintain group status quo and avoid rocking the boat.

Fist-to-five prevents skewing decisions to the most vocal, loud, and articulate meeting participants at the expense of others who aren't like that. Analytical introverts might have critical insights, yet they need the meeting air time and psychological safety to share them for everyone's benefit.

In addition to finalizing a group decision, you can use fist-to-five to check if everyone understands a given proposal.

Disagree and commit

You don't need 100% agreement in order to move ahead, as long as everyone commits to what the group decides. This is a practical insight because it can free up the team to take action sooner.

"Disagree and commit" is a useful pattern to help avoid the consensus trap, where participants don't take action because they didn't feel the group actually committed to an approach. Scott McNeally, the founder of Sun Microsystems, used the phrase as early as 1991 as part of the line, "Agree and commit, disagree and commit, or get out of the way".

Commit and take action. If it's the wrong decision, you can always cut your losses. Commit to another approach in the future based on what you learn from the first decision. At least you aren't waiting, but taking action in the meantime.

Maintain it

Once you re-establish a decent baseline of interactions across silos, it's also worth considering how you can maintain this momentum going forwards. This is easy to do with the following approaches:

Writing asynchronously

Improved documentation and clarity around how things work, ideally owned and updated by everyone and not as an implicit control mechanism for the top of the company hierarchy. More clarity like this helps reduce the need for "status meetings." In particular, if everyone is clear on exactly what is happening and how the process looks.

Tweaking meeting sequences

It's useful to think through exactly who needs to collaborate and how frequently. This will typically involve stakeholders for specific initiatives, projects, or products being worked on. Reducing the cadence, e.g. from a weekly to a monthly meeting, could free up time to do more work. Conversely, you need enough of a relationship to raise questions and concerns with one another naturally.

Visual monitoring or using dashboards

An accurate visual is worth a thousand words, and probably a hundred meetings. For example, tools like standup.ly[52] aggregate information shared during a standup into metrics and trends. There are tools to track OKRs like weekdone[53] or koan[54].

Deliberate employee sharing

ZingTrain's cross-pollination of employees across business units also broke down their silos. Originally, ZingTrain introduced this policy to fill a hiring gap on the support team. Yet, it became a company jewel because of the other benefits it yielded. It gave a useful perspective for the people in technical or administrative roles later in their careers because they had the "voice of customer" ingrained in their heads. It also gave an effective introduction to the industry for anyone completely new.

I've seen this approach work first-hand at a startup I joined out of school. Every new hire had to work for 3 months in support before moving onto their actual role. This meant that everyone-including technical staff like developers knew what customers wanted and expected. Naturally, the work done was much more effective.

The important aspect here is to communicate openly in all directions. Do not rely solely on company hierarchy as a

---

[52] https://standup.ly
[53] https://www.weekdone.com
[54] https://www.koan.co

filtering mechanism. There is an informal way employees communicate in every company. I've found it most helpful to plug into these patterns, rather than to ignore or suppress them. As a side effect, you prevent creating silos like Wernher von Braun's Monday Notes at NASA.

What this means

If you implement all the above, you will improve the company culture. Healing it of the disconnects caused by the previously mentioned cultural blender-turned-heater. It also means that you flatten or supplement the pre-existing hierarchy by starting new relationships across the company. You don't leave people to fend for themselves. They know who to ask, if they have a problem. They can tap into this in-company network of expertise if necessary.

If you achieve greater alignment, eventually work feels less stressful. Everyone knows what needs to be happening, and also they can act accordingly in the moment. There are no artificial boundaries that exist, including the inadvertently created ones. Everyone works towards the good of the company as a whole, and not just their silo. The company operates in greater alignment with its declared values. Every employee feels it. The whole becomes stronger, greater than the sum of its parts. If you align well, everyone in the company will feel good about their job. They buy into the vision and values.

At that point, it stops mattering if you work from an office or from home; where you work becomes irrelevant. These issues downgrade into a tooling question, rather than an existential one. Operationally, lack of motivation is most observable in how meetings work. Meetings are the main way employees experience company culture. More on that in the next section.

Key takeaways

- Visual process mapping, especially if it's done across functions, is the best possible tool for sense-making and reducing ambiguity.
- Go asynchronous when you can, especially around work that isn't actually urgent. Urgency as a tool to manage and motivate is short-lived.
- Make and evaluate decisions frequently using fist-to-five and "disagree and commit", especially if you are under significant time pressure. The ability to back out of a decision is more valuable than making the right decision.

https://recommendedbyluke.com/miroFishbowl for an example of a whiteboard-based approach

Section takeaways

- A useful incremental measure of alignment is how much the team members *and* leaders give the same responses to questions around what, how, and why they are doing what they are doing.
- Connecting why and how helps motivate everyone involved, so that they understand how their efforts contribute to the bigger picture.
- If successfully aligned, a team feels an emotional fuel, powering the teams to achieve strategic objectives.
- A healthy culture supports alignment. A lack of alignment in a remote-first world can motivate employees to disengage and leave for easily accessible pastures elsewhere.
- Many conflicts arise in companies because each side pays attention or notices different facts without the full context.
- Giving every stakeholder group a voice means they later have a stake in the solution and ultimate outcome.
- Usually, teams align internally; bigger challenges lie across department lines.
- Sensemaking is the best approach to breaking down silos.
- Figure out what most people are struggling with, identify the underserved value, and use it to rally your teams.

Rethinking productivity

In which our plucky narrator re-examines what productivity means-in order to find his bearings when working with remote teams.

Source: Massimo Canducci

Quick challenge ideas

Here's a few quick ideas on how to evaluate where you and your company are, in terms of productivity:

- Calculate the length of time it takes from getting a customer request or marketing idea, to when the customer sees the result. Take 1-3 recent releases, deliveries, or project completions and calculate an average.
- Write down 1-3 key metrics that you currently track or discuss during meetings with your colleagues and bosses.

So how do we know our people are working?

Hands down, this is the most common question that new remote managers have. And sadly, it's a slippery slope. A good retort is to ask back, "how do you know people are working when you're in the office?" And then consider if each of those tactics help you differentiate effectiveness from looking busy.

These questions bring to light the fact that managers monitor productivity based on proxy measures, like physical presence of employees in the office. Or utilization. They assume that having a body in an office for eight hours a day for multiple days in a row will eventually lead to an pre-agreed positive (financial) result.

Time doesn't always equal money. Also, work time doesn't always equal money. And when it does, the money earned is rarely proportional to the time a team spends together.

Understanding team time management

Arguably, "time management" itself is a misnomer for work outside of simple and repeatable work, like the work performed on a factory production line. Arguably, the whole concept comes from Frederick Winslow Taylor's early 20th century insights around optimizing factory production lines. His core assumption was that time equals money linearly, because time dictated the output produced. That model and its assumptions break down in the context of office work, particularly more creative or analytical work like software development for example.

The latter is often more like working on a farm. Regular habits and effective routines over long chunks of time, often weeks or months, results in a harvest of output. Yes you have to plant, plow, and pluck in a rough order and follow a rough timeline to have something to harvest. The hours you work in one day are irrelevant. The weather during the year can be highly relevant. You organize your time around the high-level task, rather than organize your tasks around the blocks of time available to each human resource.

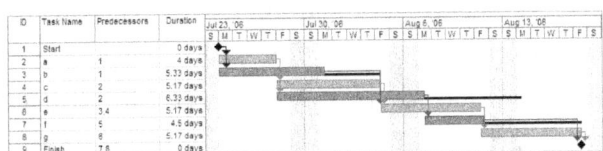

Gantt chart to plan around dependencies

Traditional project management styles have this linear assumption of time equals money embedded, for example, in tools like Gantt charts. Each team member exerts a fixed amount of effort for each task. If the team member isn't applying that effort and works the full amount of planned work time, the presumption is that the task won't be completed.

Many tools, like MS Project, attempt to create detailed schedules based on several dependencies and deadlines. While this level of detail is meant to increase trust levels in a plan, unnecessary commitment to intermediate deadlines often causes you to lose sight of underlying priorities. At best, you optimize locally, with a hefty global price tag. One project is delivered on time, causing slippage on other projects. This reduces trust in detailed plans, which then means even more detailed planning. **In MS Project, "Finish-To-Start" (FTS) task dependencies implicitly capture much of the process debt inherent in traditional project management.** It's also the default type of task dependency in MS Project. With FTS, you have to finish a certain task by a certain date, so you specify that the start date of any dependent tasks must start early enough to finish the other task on time. While this sounds like a good idea at a high level, i.e. "start with the end in mind", it creates a lot of unnecessary and unintended inflexibility at the task level. With FTS, you unknowingly commit to interim deadlines that may or may not align with your future priorities.

To be fair, thinking through task dependencies explicitly can be a useful exercise. But then, if a manager assigns a specific person to each task, he centralizes ownership and responsibility. Then it's difficult to delegate ownership for the task, and more importantly, the final outcome.

At some level, you need to put in effort to achieve a result.

But first and foremost, the desired result needs to be clear. And at most companies, it sadly isn't clear enough. Once the outcome is made clear, the team needs to own it. To figure out how to achieve it. It's better to delegate outcomes to teams. It's more fun and engaging for them.

Prescribing detailed work breakdowns at the beginning of a project can create bottlenecks, paradoxically reducing team effectiveness. Who cares if the team is efficient, if they aren't effective? In other words, leadership trumps management.

This is especially true in a highly volatile or ambiguous business environment. Leadership is a skill-set that is independent of the company hierarchy. It includes many skills that don't require hierarchy: delegation, prioritization, and empathy, for example.

Clocking in and out at the factory every day

Take prioritization for example. If there are too many

projects, typically they be perceived to have equal priority, and different deadlines. It takes a lot of extra effort to ensure that priority isn't lost in the detail. Moreover, it's easier to start and run projects than it is to finish them. The net result is often more concurrent projects than resources available, which results in a "company-wide ADHD" (attention deficit hyperactivity disorder), if I fan use that analogy. As mentioned in the chapter on leadership's role in reducing ambiguity, employees are constantly switching among project contexts. With each additional project or initiative, it becomes harder to finish the current projects already running.

Companies that relied on proxy metrics like attendance to "measure" productivity have typically not fared well in the shift to working remotely. All of the above was always true, but it was easier to cope with this efficient but ineffective operating model where everyone was in an office together. Instead of tying activity back to well-defined and prioritized goals, knowledge work managers tracked employee time spent delivering a project, to guesstimate progress. "Yep, that project is on schedule with 74% of the work completed." These types of estimates are based on subjective and potentially biased assessments, based on many assumptions, and often turn out to be wildly wrong when you are almost done, i.e. 99% there.

In particular, if the goals of the organization aren't clear, managerial incentives are inconsistent with them, or the goals don't feel relevant to the people in the company, then tactics like continuous-time tracking may be a distracting ritual. They delay getting better clarity and direction. Let's break that down, by going to first principles around accountability and delegation.

Key takeaways

- Time equals money when doing simple work, and most office work is not simple.
- Proxy productivity measures tend to focus on the individual, whereas they should be tied closer to outcomes.

Why traditional productivity measures don't add up

Corporate thinking about productivity tends to over-focus on benchmarking individual output. From an individual productivity standpoint, you benchmark individuals against a team's average output. And you see who is contributing more and less than the average. But that doesn't clarify what is really happening. Or the best next steps. All of which matter operationally.

"The defenders were there in spirit, so it's all your fault"

There is quite a mind shift awaiting when you think about productivity from a team perspective first.

Case Study: Project Aristotle at Google

Curious about what drives productivity, Google dug into an extended research project run by their People Analytics department. They dubbed the initiative "Project Aristotle" [55], referring to Aristotle's famous observation that, in some cases, the value of a whole can be greater than the sum of its parts. The researchers interviewed 115 engineering and 65 sales teams, who exhibited a wide range of effectiveness. They measured effectiveness with team output, outcomes achieved, and also revenue earned where relevant. In the process, they sussed out hundreds of variables that might explain the performance variation. Examples included demographic ones like location or seniority, as well as personality traits, skill sets, and emotional intelligence.

The researchers found that who was on the team didn't matter at Google. Their infamous grilling of candidates and recruitment of outstanding individuals from top universities had no relation to team effectiveness. How the team worked together mattered a lot more. In particular, the following variables explained the performance the most:

1. *Psychological safety*: Whether team members felt comfortable expressing what they thought or taking a risk, particularly risks that would make a team

---

[55] https://recommendedbyluke.com/ProjectAristotle

member look bad before the other team members.
2. *Dependability*: All team members strove to complete their work on time.
3. *Structure and clarity*: Team members were clear on both their expectations of them and the process for fulfilling those expectations.
4. *Meaning*: Whether team members found meaning in the work itself mattered quite a bit.
5. *Impact*: The feeling that the work creates positive organizational change or change for customers also mattered.

These findings give leaders a clear picture of what needs to be in place for individuals to feel empowered to do everything they can for their teams. Doing a gap analysis relative to your current situation against these criteria gives you a clear sense of how you can improve productivity on your teams. This is true regardless of where they work physically: office, remote, or hybrid.

Also, this list gives a clear picture of how relationships at work "should" look. Instead of getting lost in platitudes and jargon, the above translate to specific lines of inquiry you can pursue when trying to improve performance, both in technology and outside of tech, as the sales teams serve as a proxy for non-technical white-collar work. This way, you know what to look for.

Key takeaways

- Team productivity explains overall output better than

individual productivity, with major implications across hiring and management practices.
- At a team level, not all tasks, resources, and even outcomes matter equally when tracking productivity.
- Team level measures are more accurate ways to track what is happening and also let the team take responsibility for their results.

What we've got here is a failure to delegate

According to Slack's 2019 State of Work survey, [56] knowing "who" is responsible for "what" was a major struggle for employees before the pandemic:

1. More transparency across the company
2. More cross-team collaboration
3. *Clear documentation around who is responsible for what*
4. Open access to leadership
5. *Clear processes around who makes what decision*

In items 3 and 5, employees beg for better delegation, clarity, and accountability. Moreover, it's fair to say that alignment in larger companies was weak, which corresponds with low levels of engagement and motivation consistently shown in many corporate surveys. Since then, a pandemic exacerbated the problems by sending everyone home for years.

As a leader, if you don't define and agree on which "who" is responsible for each "what," then everyone else won't be clear on it. When holding a group of people

---

[56] https://recommendedbyluke.com/SlackStateofWork

accountable, things get murky quickly. In the absence of in-person communication, delegation suddenly becomes more difficult (and it's hard enough to delegate in person already). This is true of a team leader. It's true of interpersonal accountability on the team. It's true of accountability between teams or functional areas.

Delegating effectively is a core leadership skill, regardless of whether you are in-person or remote. Once you delegate work or decisions, the teams affected also need to know who owns what. The reality is that, as leaders, we often don't delegate well even in person:

1. We think we have set a clear expectation or standard, and we have not.
2. We think we have given real-time feedback, and we have not.
3. We think we have established clear consequences for action/inaction, and we have not.
4. We think our standards are clear to employees, but they are not.
5. We think it's obvious how to apply our standards to any situation, but they are not.

Unless we are deliberately paying close attention to all of this (and trying to catch it when it happens), we often miss these slip-ups.

We are trying to delegate in an environment where we haven't been understood. We haven't made the effort to fully understand the other person's perspective. The latter is necessary, to articulate the consequences of delegatee action or inaction—whatever they choose to do. This mismatch becomes blatantly obvious when going remote. In an office, we could rely on coping strategies and feedback we used in the past, like non-verbal communication. Without direct contact, delegation can blow up in our face.

Healthy accountability

Accountability is strictly tied with outcome clarity. It means you are willing to answer for the outcomes and consequences resulting from your team's actions. In other words, you step up and tie good and bad outcomes to your own or your team's actions. This means that a focus on results is joint at the hip with a focus on clear intended outcomes, which in turn, is joint at the hip to accountability, which in turn relates to your actions.

> results <- outcomes <- actions <- accountability

When you hold yourself personally accountable, you take ownership of situations you're involved in. You see them through. At the same time, you expect the follower to own it. You help them if they struggle, without pre-packaging solutions for them.

It's important to note that there are many styles of accountability. Bullying and threatening people is at one end of the spectrum; supportive coaching accountability is at the other. The latter is a lot harder. It requires self-awareness, so that you don't devolve to the former.

When you coach, you define plans together with your coachees. In this case, the coachees understand the wider context and hold themselves accountable, because they understand the consequences of their actions.

With high accountability, you don't blame others if things go wrong. "Blame is just the discharge of discomfort and pain. It is the inverse of accountability," according to Brene Brown. You forgive. It's hard if the problem is something that matters to you. Instead, you do your best to make things right. In my own experience, it was much faster to jump instinctively towards blame, anger, and control when someone disappointed me rather than to feel grief. And to forgive while making space to discuss consequences and taking accountability as a team.

It's up to the leader to confront issues without assigning blame or punishment, by working through and resolving them. **In other words, the leader needs to make space for the follower to fail, which can be hard.**

Managers who like to hoard ownership and responsibility feel it immediately reflects poorly on them if an employee messes up. Of course, you want to prevent what you can. But if the follower doesn't mess up, they won't ever feel ownership. Or accountability. It's easier for them to just let the manager deal with it, and do the job for them.

I struggled with this when starting to manage software

developers. I wanted the product to be well built according to the standard I held myself accountable for. During initial planning, I got a reasonably clear picture of how it was going to work, and tried to force my co-workers into adopting it. Which they found demotivating. As I was less and less involved in the actual work, the truth was that my technical skills were "half-life'ing" anyway, due to the rapid pace of change. I realized that it was my job to define what needed to be done and why at a high level. And then to step away. It made my job a little more manageable, and I also made space for the team to go in and build great product. In fact, better than I would be able to by then anyway.

Accounting for time spent within an organizational structure

Organizational structures themselves can undermine accountability. The truth is accountability must be two-way, if you want to give it a chance. By default, there needs to be a clear one-to-one relationship between a manager and their employee. If you have multiple projects and partial allocations, there are also easy traps to fall into. And ultimately, the organizational structure is the responsibility of a leader somewhere in the company hierarchy. Then it is easy to hold one another accountable.

In matrix organizational structures, each employee will have multiple managers. This can seem like a good idea when organizing work, but you lose clear lines of accountability when choosing to go in this direction. It becomes the employee's responsibility to get the managers to agree by default. If they disagree, then at least one of the managers will be unhappy. This environment implicitly means any leader can easily abdicate responsibility, sometimes even not consciously.

Conversely, partial allocations to projects make it hard to hold anyone accountable, with percentage allocations of employee time to various efforts; it's hard enough with 100% allocations. You are assuming several things which have to hold true to maintain accountability:

- The employee is accurately noting down their time based on how much they spend on each project.
- The employee is inputting their time regularly enough that it is relatively accurate and not on a monthly or quarterly basis.
- There is no overlap among the projects; where something is done once it is relevant for more than one project.
- Employees have no personal preferences or motivations that would influence how much they like one project, client, or manager over another, thus possibly causing them to bias their time reporting.
- You assume there is no cognitive cost of multi-tasking, which statistically doesn't hold up according to various studies.
- There can be a disconnect between how much an employee enters and how much is agreed on upfront among the managers of a target time spent, as well

as how much each relevant project or department manager perceives, based on the employee's outputs.

So as you can see, there are many hurdles in a partial allocation environment for employees who genuinely want to stay accountable for their work (and most do).

Using this approach creates many situations that can subtly undermine confidence that the employee is productive. It can devolve into a game of employees guessing "what I can get away with" and managing the expectations gap. In certain contexts, this level of timekeeping is inevitable and necessary. For example, employee expert time is the "product" in a consulting or professional services department. Or you have to have a matrix structure and can't have a flatter hierarchy. This is ok, as long as everyone acknowledges this kind of structure subtly undermines employees from truly owning their results.

If accountability isn't two-way, it's easy for the relevant managers to distrust the data, start fighting among each other, and ultimately treating the employee as a resource to be exploited. But nobody wants to be treated like an oil field.

In a larger organization, accountability naturally becomes more complicated and intertwined. It's distributed among a lot of people. And it also depends on the culture and systems in which it operates. I'd venture that if organizational accountability doesn't exist, it's because it's insufficiently bi-directional. Essentially both the leader and the follower need to be willing to agree and subject themselves to an external standard:

- This standard should be unambiguous and apply to both.
- It should also be clear to both why it's necessary.
- The follower can always opt-out of the standard by leaving, even if they don't participate in the process of defining it. And sadly, they often do.
- The leader is responsible for the patterns and the system, so if something is repeatedly wrong, that's on the leader.

Unfortunately, the details of how to increase accountability in your company will depend on company-specific factors.

Accountability that works

In order to delegate effectively, you need a baseline of accountability with yourself. In my opinion, you need to hold yourself accountable before you can hold someone else accountable. If you don't hold yourself accountable for what you say, the people around you see that. Even kids can pick up hypocrisy at a young age. Of course, this is a high bar but a necessary one if you want to systematically delegate ownership.

Author Jonathan Raymond defines delegation as "passing accountability for an outcome to another person." His book *The Good Authority* introduces an excellent framework for accountability at work called the Accountability Dial. Ideally, accountability balances with kindness, according to Jonathan Raymond. The mindset assumes that delegated work is important to the employee (otherwise they wouldn't be in their career). The manager's role is "to help you make sure you do it [for your own benefit and that of the company]."

If that person doesn't live in accordance with that priority, you serve as a coach giving tough love to help keep someone on track. The approach strikes a good balance between being a pushover who avoids conflict, thus letting the problem fester, and bullying and manipulating people into doing things your way. For example, when you see a behavior you don't like, you say something like, "I saw that. What's going on for you?".

If a problem doesn't get resolved, there are four conversations to have here for each offender, asking for their ideas on how to fix an accountability problem:

1. Notice the problem and discuss the implications for everyone.
2. If it continues, notice a pattern of the problem, and discuss implications for the business.
3. If it still continues, establish a performance improvement plan.
4. Suggest they leave the company as it is not a good fit.

This way, you will be respectful while still holding them

accountable. And in many regulatory jurisdictions, you need to have documented proof of attempts to correct behavior before letting people go, so you get that as a nice extra if you take notes with each conversation.

Other tips

- Startups tend to have high accountability, and they achieve this with a particular division of labor. In *The Founder's Dilemmas* by Noah Wasserman, each person is a dictator in their area, outlined via a contract beforehand. If you're in charge of it, you get the final say. With a clear division of labor comes clear accountability: Everyone can see who is responsible for each success and failure, at least for those tasks or milestones that fit into a particular domain. In other words, anyone can help. The work happens in a company context. But it's also clear who has the final say and is responsible for an outcome.
- In established companies, high engagement cultures hold managers accountable by rewarding them for engaging with the team. According to Gallup, "Tolerance of mediocrity does not exist in the best organizations. They define high team performance based on metrics such as productivity, retention rates, customer service and employee engagement. It is clear to those managers that their job is to engage their teams." [57]

---

[57] https://recommendedbyluke.com/GallupMediocrity

- There is an old technique in software development called pair programming that can be useful in a knowledge work context. Having two people work on a task simultaneously significantly increases the quality of the work. And paradoxically speed to the outcome. As a side effect, the workers share knowledge, apply standards, and constantly provide each other feedback as they go. Having people from different functional areas within a company helps break down silos, shares knowledge, and increases collaboration. But most importantly, in this context, both sides of the pair hold each other accountable. And they improve the culture as they produce the intended outcomes with higher quality and reliability.

Key takeaways

- The move to remote has exposed a leadership skills gap where employees are managed using proxy metrics like attendance and utilization rather than being held accountable for clear customer-driven outcomes.
- If you want to enable teams to self-organize, outcomes need to be tracked at a team level, not against individual performance.
- Supportive accountability respects everyone involved: being kind and far. Bullying and manipulating people into doing their job doesn't work eventually.
- When delegating a task or an outcome, make sure you have:

1. Set a clear expectation or standard.
2. Established clear consequences for action/inaction.
3. Explained how to apply company standards to the situation.
4. Give real-time feedback, both positive and corrective.
5. If there are problems, ask the employee to articulate the standard and why it exists to diagnose where the problem lies.

The wolf you feed

> A village elder is talking with his grandson.
>
> The grandfather says, "In life, there are two wolves inside of us which are always at battle.
>
> One is a good wolf which represents things like kindness, bravery, and love.
>
> The other is a bad wolf which represents things like greed, hatred, and fear".
>
> The grandson stops and thinks about it for a second then he looks up at his grandfather and says, "Grandfather, which one wins?"
>
> The grandfather replies, "The one you feed."

What you pay attention to matters. As in the Cherokee parable above, if you focus on what makes you afraid, you end up nursing the fearful wolf. If you focus on what you want, like the bravery to pursue a market opportunity by setting a clear outcome you wish to pursue, you feed the good wolf.

The same applies to managing teams: if your metrics track resources that you're afraid of wasting, like employee time, at best you have a highly efficient workforce driven by fear. If you define exciting outcomes that pull together teams across the company, then you are much more likely to achieve them.

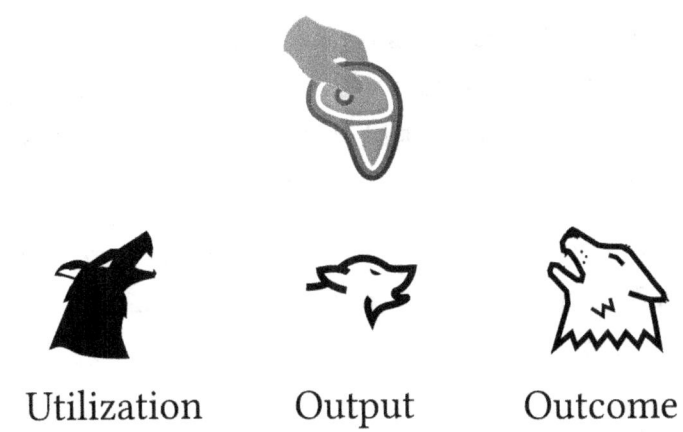

What do you talk about during meetings?

In truth, the cause-effect relationship between utilization and productivity is tenuous for complex work. Like software development. Or creative work. Or any work requiring analysis. Take a look at this video by Henrik Kniberg, [58] or look up "The resource utilization trap" on YouTube. In short, the higher your utilization of resource, the lower your output.

There are many physical analogies in the real world. How well does your laptop work when 100% of the CPU is being used? Even if it's not at 100%, your laptop stalls if it frequently hits that limit. By focussing on utilization as your core metric, you risk doing the same with your teams.

The metrics you use to "manage" the ones you focus on

---

[58] https://recommendedbyluke.com/KnibergResourceUtil

the most incentivize the workforce. And they can easily incentivize the wrong behaviors and drive the delivery and executive team's attention to the wrong things. Let me be clear, it's worthwhile to think through your objectives, key results, and metrics to implement your strategy. That usually takes a lot of honesty, courage, and self-awareness as an organization if you can do it.

Depending on how far you get in this process, you'll end up with an approach that primarily rests on one of the three categories:

1. Utilization
2. Output
3. Outcome

Usually, if you are operating from the perspective of one of these, all of the other metrics you use will be used to figure out the implications for that. They are each a different system of metrics, with different underlying assumptions about what needs to be monitored and trusted. And who, if anyone. Almost completely different philosophies, even though they are all intended to do roughly the same thing: help managers run efficient and effective companies that implement the organization's strategy. Let's dig deeper into what these mean in practice, shall we?

Utilization

A guy I used to work with a lot, moved through the ranks and became a development manager. Let's call him Ted.

Every time I'd walk over to Ted's desk or speak with him at the pub, he'd say he was busy. "Keeping busy". "We're really busy," he'd say of his team. It was almost a badge of honor, a way for him to try to earn respect from anyone who spoke to him.

In practice, it also meant that anyone who wanted to give him more to do started doubting if it made sense to do so. If he and his team are already busy, they won't have much capacity to look at what you wanted to ask about. So you end up asking someone else.

Note that he'd learned over time that it's best to say and look like he's busy, regardless of whether that was true.

He was and is a great guy to have a beer with. So I was puzzled by his behavior. And I realized that it reflected the management system in place.

If resource utilization was one of the main numbers executives asked about, then it made sense that "the management system" expected him and his team to be busy. Because that is the underlying assumption of effectiveness in this context: if all workers are at or near their capacity, then the company is correctly resourced. So capital is being used effectively.

This approach could arguably work, if the following were true:

- Every unit of output needs to adhere to a well-defined standard.
- What needs to be done is well understood, as it's been done many times before.

- The staff can be quickly trained up, and therefore are "fungible" or easily substitutable for one other.

Fungibility depends somewhat on the type of labor. Like in a factory, the official classification for unskilled vs. skilled manufacturing labor is half a day of training. If you can get a new hire up to speed within four hours, they are considered unskilled and don't cost much to replace. If they are skilled, it takes longer. However, you can assign responsibility to people relatively quickly to new hires. This mindset, or set of metrics, envisions the company operating as a factory.

It's a useful analogy if you are primarily concerned with optimizing worker output, as Frederick Winslow Taylor was. The argument goes that the whole company or department is efficient, when its sub-parts are efficient. By squeezing as much as you can out of the individual resources you have, you achieve the best possible outcome. Or so it seems.

The truth is that this mindset causes several downsides when applied to knowledge work. It's paradoxically challenging to hold any individual accountable in this context, even though this approach purportedly focuses on keeping individuals efficient. For example, a lot of effort is required to coddle, coax, and push workers to actually do the work. Because the whole system assumes that some percentage of them aren't working, it's the manager's responsibility to deploy his resources.

Managing individuals' time becomes the unit of account.

For example, you need to keep track of things like the remaining total work days before a release. Or comparing units of resources that are being allocated, and comparing them to the actual contribution of the individual. In my opinion, only tracking utilization can easily breed a distrust of line workers at the coal face. Because they will usually behave differently than what is in the top-down plan for what they are supposed to do. But this is denying one of the critical elements of human nature: the knowing-doing gap. Just because people know what is expected of them, and their livelihood depends on it, doesn't mean they will act accordingly. Classic managerial big idea books, like Daniel Pink's *Drive*, have documented this in detail, trying to popularize what has been known in academic circles since the 1960s.

In turn, at a managerial level, this type of environment makes it seemingly easy to multi-task, by allocating resources to different projects simultaneously. You move resources around on a spreadsheet. As a short-term workaround, you allocate resources to multiple projects to address various urgent issues. Often where they need to juggle multiple tasks, expectations, and often taskmasters. So if there are any unresolved conflicts at a more strategic level, you can ask any given employee to spend 20% of his time on this new project and 20% on another one. This means this also needs to be monitored and accounted for. And often, any problems end up being blamed on the workers and their character traits, instead of the fact they are being served unclear expectations.

Paradoxically, this results in a reduced focus on finishing and delivering work. Lots of multi-tasking results in having lots of planes in the air and not landing. At the same time, all of your resources are maxed out. So they don't have much capacity to change what they're doing or add to their workload. Accountability is tough to enforce. The available resources are over-committed already—by design.

Output

What's the alternative? It turns out "managing the unfinished work, and not the workers" is a better approach, as Don Reinertsen posits in *The Principles of Product Development Flow*.

The main problem with primarily focusing on resource utilization is that it's inversely related to system output, over and above a certain threshold value. This is an attribute of complex systems. If you've ever had a slow laptop, usually this is because one of the key resources it uses is maxed out. Or consistently close to the 100% mark. Either you need to add more or better resources. Or you need to change how the system works in the first place and remove the bottleneck. This is just as true within entire companies as it is on your laptop.

The above video is a compelling demonstration of this principle. Having a lot of balls in the air and many people to manage it isn't a good use of resources, regardless of how much or how few resources you have. This is what happens if you take the utilization approach too seriously to heart. Conversely, you can't completely ignore utilization either, as you can end up with problems like systemic under-staffing or individual performance issues. It's just that the primary framework to evaluate performance is in the overall output.

This is an initial step in the direction of "beginning with the end in mind." You have a goal. To achieve that goal, you need a certain amount of output. This can be measured in physical or digital terms (stories and story points). Your aim is to design a system that maximizes the rate of output. Or the change in output over the change in time. In high school calculus terms:

$d(Output)/dt$

Or velocity. Or time between releases, as Steve Jobs pointed out. It's a powerful metric that has major implications for any project or initiative, as discussed here.

The subtle shift here is that you start looking at your company as a system designed to produce output. And that system is run by delivery teams at the lowest level, not individuals. High output is achieved by finishing quickly or finishing what you start, not long after you start it. There are usually several skill sets and work processing stages involved for a specific unit of output. So you start looking at how each unit of eventual output goes from the very beginning to the end, and measuring the elapsed time it takes to achieve that. Once you do this, you rapidly realize that the units of output spend the majority of their time in-between processing states. So even if the workers are very efficient at doing their job at any given intermediate stage, it's largely irrelevant. Because the unfinished output spends disproportionately more time between stages. Or individual workers, each of which have different skill sets and talents they bring to the work.

If you do shift to thinking about time to completion for individual units of work, everything else becomes easier or unnecessary. Because you can quickly complete anything you set out to do, you become unstoppable. If no one else is doing this, you will quickly become a leader in your industry. You stop fearing competition, because you can out-execute them once your edge is big enough.

As a side effect of focusing on the overall system, you'll see a greater emergence of teamwork. Because you aren't that interested in measuring individuals, you shift the emphasis and incentives. After the initial gains of moving towards this approach, further gains in output will come from teamwork. How quickly a unit of work is passed through each stage and the type of expertise needed to complete it. Plus, it's a fun environment to work in. People aren't just punching the clock anymore. They acknowledge their interdependence with other members of the team. And you can see the effect of team dynamics on how much elapsed time is wasted in between steps–for example between development and QA.

Eventually, this approach starts to break down too, especially in a digital context. You start to hit a wall once you fully acknowledge that cognitive effort and business value are independent. Sometimes, something hard to make is valuable, and sometimes, it isn't. And vice versa. **The best example of this disconnect is the most common reason for new product failure: building something nobody wants.** In other words, you can construct a high output system that spends a lot of time building irrelevant or un-finish-able things. Together with this, consider that not all units of output matter equally, especially in a digital context. For example, in software, if you build and release one highly relevant feature that directly solves a big problem for your customers, it can have a lot of value. To keep it simple, a big B2B customer has 45% cost savings of some sort by implementing your one-feature solution. If you then go and build another big feature or prioritize the work correctly, the next feature down will have less of an impact on the same customer. So it will have less value, even though it requires roughly the same amount of work.

At its core, if you are truly producing units of output frequently, this is why "scope creep" doesn't matter as much when you are focused on velocity. Yes, there are a lot of things you could do. And this increases. But the individual stories or features will have different levels of business value. If you release as early as possible and not when everything is ready, you are in a better place to start having sales discussions earlier. This is the whole selling point of focusing on completion instead of utilization.

Outcomes

The real point of productivity isn't really to finish lots of output. The real point is to achieve what you care about quickly. But then it means you need to be clear on the outcomes you're trying to achieve in the first place. And I mean crystal clear. Usually this isn't in place. Everyone defaults to focusing on outputs or managing resources. It will vary a lot by which person you ask in a new product development environment. It can be a bit overwhelming for people who are totally new at this, but eventually it can be twisted into something useful. I find that it will be used in a different context than originally prototyped.

After all, new product development is messy. When you first start on anything that's truly new, you don't have a clue on what success looks like. You have a lot of hopes and some guesses, but that's probably it. Pretending it's not only makes it a lot harder.

Beyond that, you need to go and speak to customers in greater depth to figure out what they look like and what they care about. There are many tools that help you investigate this whole space. Teresa Torres (@ttorres) has her outcome-based trees to help explore a given space where you're totally new, summarized in *Continuous Discovery Habits*. Gojko Adzic (@gojkoadzic) came up with the impact map concept, where you brainstorm outcomes per stakeholder, in his aptly titled *Impact Mapping*. And then map them together in a workshop format ideally.

Ultimately, these outcomes are tied to the value proposition box on the Business Model Canvas you are working with. These are the benefits that your prospects will care about. So how you do it (in terms of solution) is not that important–to them. They only care about the outcome. They "hire" your product to achieve that outcome. In the same way that you own and use a car to get from point a to point b. Most people won't care about the engine or horsepower or anything specific to building a car from scratch. This is because it's a relatively mature market and the technology has been well understood for a while.

For example, I recently read a post-mortem of a failed HR software startup: Ansaro. [59] In short, there were a lot of reasons why they struggled, but one item in particular stuck out to me:

> The problem we set out to tackle, reducing turnover and improving new hire performance, was felt acutely by our buyers (CHROs / Heads of Talent). It was NOT felt acutely by our users (recruiters).
>
> **Recruiters are measured against average time-to-hire, not new hire retention or performance.**

They were trying to improve outcomes about which users would pay lip service, but which didn't impact their paychecks or promotions. They had focused on the wrong metric (outcome) because they focused on the buyer's

---
[59] https://recommendedbyluke.com/AnsaroPostMortem

needs, not the user's needs. The buyer wants an overall outcome. The users just want to be able to move through the software quickly, to achieve the operational outcome expected. It's a case of building a product that achieved the wrong thing. In other words, they'd built the wrong features, or at least insufficient features, to be able to get the result that the customer wanted.

It was especially difficult because it was a B2B sale with multiple stakeholders at a client site. But ultimately, the delivery velocity didn't matter, because they didn't focus on the right value propositions and metrics that the prospects cared about. So their product failed.

And it's a mistake to think that these are separate things (effect from delivery process). It's tempting to keep them separate in different silos at a company. But you'll get more mileage by making sure that, for example, the developers understand the customer's pain, so that they will be able to take any customer constraints into consideration as they build and prototype the solution. If you think it's a question of forcing the team to build faster, you increase the risk of building something totally irrelevant.

But when I'm starting out, I don't know what outcomes matter...

That's exactly why it's a mistake to focus primarily on utilization or even output metrics, until you have better validation and structure around what matters on a new project or product. And what you want to achieve. Even if you think you need a lot of "building" to happen first. It's possible to try working on all three levels with your team.

That may be a smart move if you are keen on timing the release relative to other things going on.

That's it in a nutshell.

Ideally, operate on all three levels. And clarify them from the outcomes back down to the resource utilization.

1. It should be clear what the stakeholders and goals are, so that you can start building things.
2. Once you do that, make sure that your team has clear output targets (and keep the releases as small as possible).
3. Only then, do you start looking at the "feature factory" efficiency measures.

Established companies often default to a feature factory approach, because that's what they know and understand well. But then it can mean they are like a forlorn babe in the woods with their new product efforts, which require constant re-prioritization as you learn and discover new target outcomes.

If you prioritize an end-to-end view, ideally including sales and marketing from the beginning when defining outcomes, it helps significantly to avoid silos, with all of the implications on team motivation mentioned earlier.

Key takeaways

- Utilization is often a default way of looking at corpo-

rate productivity, because it permits decision-makers to avoid aligning around outcomes while still looking and feeling like everyone is 'productive'.
- Manage productivity with outcomes first, then output, and finally look at resource utilization, in order to get the greatest value from the resources you have.

Given outcomes, teams can manage their own work

When managing remote teams, I quickly realized the importance of prioritizing team-produced outcomes. By focusing on outcomes, you understand the team's dynamic and help them achieve as a group. My primary remit was speed. When they truly acted as a team, they were fast. For example, this meant jumping in to help one another to achieve a larger goal or complete a task on the critical path. They all needed enough ownership and context to make those decisions among themselves.

Team productivity outweighs individual productivity

Ideally, these outcomes tie back to the company's strategic goals and values, which requires a dose of self-awareness from everyone in the company.

Lacking that, it's possible to work on a smaller scale.

You can create such an environment for individual delivery teams as an initial step if necessary. Admittedly, there was a lot of emphasis on individual or functional department performance among my fellow managers. In contrast, I focused intensely on how team dynamics contributed to outcomes. Anything else only mattered if it slowed down or blocked the team from hitting their goals.

Surprisingly, this included individual performance, which is often where traditional performance management starts and ends. While individual performance is important, it's much less important than providing the right context for adults to work. I focused on managing the work before focusing on managing the workers. This meant really focusing on what was being done. It meant identifying and clearing all bottlenecks or blockers.

Commander's intent

The core unit of currency is the intended outcome. In the US military, itself a rather complicated organization, they use the term "commander's intent". Helio Fred Garcia summarizes in *The Power of Communication*:

> Marines follow orders, but not blindly. Commander's intent is an essential part of an order. Understanding a commander's intent is the responsibility of each Marine. And making that intent clear is the responsibility of each commander, of whatever rank.

This simple building block helps them act appropriately, even in an unpredictable environment like a battlefield. But it also works back at HQ. Most problems arise when that intent isn't articulated, clear, or understood.

By defining the high-level outcome you want to achieve, you give your team space. Achieving the commander's intent can become an inherently motivating game—any game type, not just a first-person shooter.

Don't tell people what to do. Tell them:

1. What not to do, and
2. What they're trying to achieve, and
3. Let them figure out how to do it

You want people to be creative, because that's what's most motivating. The commander's intent becomes a creative constraint, allowing people to experiment productively. It's motivating and inspiring. It also frees you up. The team knows what is important to you, so you don't need to dig into all of the details yourself as a leader.

ROWE

Without knowing what it was called, I had inadvertently created a results-only work environment [60] or ROWE[61]. Jody Thompson and Cali Ressler pioneered ROWE at Best Buy, a consumer goods retailer, in the early 2000s.

---

[60] https://recommendedbyluke.com/ROWEDefinition
[61] https://www.gorowe.com

By moving away from attendance measures and flexible work options, Thompson and Ressler realized that the traditional mindset and metrics were counterproductive. Once business goals were truly clear at all levels, these attempts at smiling towards employees while minimizing negative impact disappeared. If everyone:

1. Knew what the goals were
2. Agreed to them together
3. Made visible progress

Then, managers didn't need to treat team members like schoolchildren. The team members could decide for themselves how to work to achieve the team's goals, usually resulting in greater efficiency than a micro-manager could squeeze out of the team.

If ROWE works in high-touch retail, it's worth a shot in white collar work

ROWE hailed from retail, an industry that relies on being in-person. Clients and co-workers expect high-touch interactions, where the business relationship involves frequent and personalized interactions, typically physically and in person. But ROWE itself doesn't require high touch and works well with remote teams.

Here's an analogy from Jody Thompson of ROWE fame:

> If I said, "we're all going to go on a trip tomorrow, meet me at nine o'clock in the morning." What would be the first thing you'd need to know? You have to know where we're going. Okay. So let's pretend you think we're going to ski in the Swiss Alps, but we're really going to Hawaii on the beach. So you pack all the wrong things. You spend a lot of time with your activity. You pack your bags, you bring your skis, you're all ready to go and you get to the airport. And I [say], 'we're going to the beach'. So when you've wasted a lot of time. The team that does the reservations for everybody, they have us going to 50 different places because they didn't understand where we were going. It's already at 9:00 AM. And so all we knew was get there at nine.

Re-alignment is the first step in moving to work remotely, so that teams stay effective to make up for any losses in efficiency. Morale stays high when everyone's motivations remain synchronized; high morale means you win big as a company. When transitioning to remote teams, remember that every team member has their own needs and motivations, as well as both a unique yet incomplete

Understanding of overall company goals, You need to align peopl's goals first. Also, the competing goals of specific roles or depart ments. This is even more critical in a distributed enviroment, where you can't rely on typical sources of feedback. In short, you need to direct everyone's attention and motivation correctly if you are gunning for high performance in a remote team.

9am the next morning

- In my particular case, this approach worked well for out team for several reasons:

- They were highly skilled and motivated, so it made sense to treat them like adults.

- We openly discussed the outcomes needed, so they had enough context to contribute meaningfully to strategy and apply it to daily work

- I let them enjoy the fun of figuring out how to achieve the goals.

- We were already pretty distributed, so the situation forced me to trust that they were actively engaging with work.

- There were several introverts on the team, so giving them space boosted their productivity,

- Senior leaders agreed to leave the team allocated full-time to our product over an extended period, so thankfully, I didn't need to deal with external resource conflicts.

I didn't track availability, staffing levels, or vacations because this would be overhead detracting from the creative process and didn't matter because the team wasn't externally facing.

- Everyone (myself included) could deal with personal issues, sick children, or inconvenient commutes easily throughout the day and didn't need to ask for permission.

- We shipped, and eventually, we became fast thanks to clearing a lot of contextual bottlenecks.

Most importantly, the approach worked! In my opinion, the role of a knowledge work manager is to create a safe context where it is easy for employees to learn and achieve goals on behalf of the company. In developing a new product, learning was our chief bottleneck. I served as a facilitator, more than a manager. I exposed and prioritized problems and then let the team figure out how to solve them. I realized I was using lightweight group psychology, similar to the pedagogy of a college classroom. This approach translated well into a remote knowledge work context, too.

"This is your last warning-either you act like you're psychologically safe, or you're fired!"

Surprisingly, employees—especially good ones—are keen on ROWEs. They're happy to take ownership and responsibility for results, if it means eliminating bureaucratic overhead like entering timesheets. Jody Thompson quips:

> It's amazing what teams come up with when they're presented with the idea that we're not going to measure your time anymore. We're not going to measure if you're available. We're not going to measure how busy you are. We're actually going to measure the work. People get really excited about that. 'OK, I'm free, but I'm getting paid for actually proving out a measurable result. Not only myself, but my team.'

My experience, so far, has been the same.

Key takeaways

- An intended outcome is the most important unit of accountability for delivery teams.
- Employees are keen to work towards results, as it usually means they have greater autonomy.

How to apply a team lens to output

Here are three ways to think about how teams can produce more valuable output:

1. Output is delivered once the last team delivers the product or service to the customer. Team-produced results are closer to the customer's experience of your products and services. Customers don't care about individual performance. Therefore, a customer perspective gives you more accurate criteria for operational decisions.
2. At a team level, not all tasks, resources, and even outcomes matter equally. Instead of losing this information to benchmarking averages, use it to your advantage.
3. Also, teams are better at optimizing their downtime relative to output than anyone who wants to micromanage how they spend their time. For most types of office-based work, output is not linearly related to the number of hours spent in front of a monitor. It's more complicated than that.

1. A task matters based on how much it affects customers

Shift towards how the customer perceives that work to help you prioritize it. If everyone is busy doing something the customer never experiences, it's difficult to know if the effort is productive. Of course, it still costs as much as being productive, but you don't have anything to show for it. It might be a symptom of the company struggling under the weight of its own bureaucracy.

Using the customer's perspective as a filter for priority

Instead, orient output so that customers receive it quickly and can provide feedback to co-create solutions with you. Make sure your expenses lead to ideal products for customers. In practice, this means focusing on how quickly teams work and span department boundaries. Because that is usually how you can dramatically decrease wait times, improve accuracy, and often improve quality, too.

By "customer", this can mean both current customers or prospective future customers or market segments. While anyone can potentially be a client, it will often be customers in the same industry or existing paying customers. For businesses, customer focus is the key concept to optimizing company productivity. Everything boils down to demand in a business context. So if customers don't need the particular thing being created, and are both willing and able to pay for it, then it's irrelevant. This singular focus on customer value is absolutely critical.

This is much more important than efficiency to help window-dress your financial results at a project or a company level. If you are efficiently doing something that nobody cares about, you are wasting 100% of the resources allocated to it.

2. The $10,000/hour question

Even when we focus on what a particular person is doing, productivity is quite slippery. Your core business contains everything you can do better and cheaper than anyone else; hand over everything else to suppliers or partners, so they deliver it for you. If it's related to your core business, it has high value for your customers. Delegate or stop doing everything else. Ideally, you want each employee to be working where they produce highly valuable output for customers. As high as possible.

> Tom DeMarco said it best in the classic book *People-Ware*: "Productivity ought to mean achieving more in an hour of work, but all too often it has come to mean extracting more for an hour of pay."

There are two sides to this problem:

1. Is the company providing a valuable product or service, one for which customers are happy to pay decent money? Or buy frequently, so the company can earn a decent margin?
2. Is the distribution of work within the company accurate and optimal, given labor market rates and final output prices?

The first question is strategic and has more to do with big picture factors such as unmet demand on the customer side. It affects who you hire and how many people you hire. It's not related to how teams execute day-to-day.

In contrast, the second one is a useful filter for work breakdown and distribution. For example, this principle applies to assigning individual tasks. This is Perry Marshall's idea of estimating the market value of a task, when deciding who does what. Any given task can be worth roughly ten dollars an hour on the open market, versus one hundred, versus a thousand, versus ten thousand.

And this uneven "perceived value" of work is a really useful mindset, as you are sorting through different types of work. It helps you figure out what is a valuable use of time for everyone.

Which side of the desk do you want to be on...the $10/hour work or the $10,000/hour work?

It also applies when the team distributes tasks among themselves. Think about how valuable a given task is. And then, as a team, make sure that whoever picks up the task is playing to their strengths, interests, and skills. Sometimes, the senior people need to be freed up to do big picture creative visioning by having the less experienced people do the necessary but less exciting work. Sometimes, a highly motivated junior can outperform someone with more experience but less enthusiasm and motivation. And sometimes, it's better to delegate the task out of the team, or even out of the company, and pay someone external to complete a simple task, like transcription, for example. Because you know it costs $1/minute, and a senior exec's time is worth a lot more than $60/hour.

A common anti-pattern: senior executives doing work with low financial value. They could easily outsource or delegate those tasks to a smart person with less experience, given enough context. For example, in small companies, founders often feel the temptation to do everything, to keep actual financial costs down. Yet their average effective hourly rate of the founders' time stays low. If they need to mop the floors or fix every technical problem on a website, they don't have time or energy to engage with customers and dream up new products or marketing campaigns. In effect, there is a very real opportunity cost to such an approach. Not to mention, it means that the founders always have to work in the business and it never becomes a source of passive income.

The trap here is only using effort-particularly its cost-to prioritize work. It doesn't matter (to customers) how much effort you need to exert to complete a task. Digging ditches or pouring cement takes a lot of effort, as I know from working as a gardener during my teenage years. Yet these tasks are not likely to be valued by anyone at ten thousand dollars an hour. Although, to be fair, government contracting might be an option for you.

In contrast, work that plays to an individual's strengths—and is very unique—will probably be quite valuable for the right customer. If you are tapping into your unique talents, experience and existing business relationships, combining them into a powerful experience, it will be highly valuable in certain customers' eyes.

This approach frees the team to hand out tasks based on their ability to contribute, while still having a market-based yardstick to rationalize the allocation economically. It results in a better distribution of work across a group of people. It's a better criterion than only relying on "effort spent". But it requires you to have a strong customer focus and tie that back into specific priorities for the team which they can go off and execute individually. So looping back to Tom DeMarco's angle, it's best to have each individual working on the highest value tasks possible in the moment (most tied to potential future sales), and not limit performance management to paying people as little as you can.

3. Energy management trumps time management

Jim Loehr and Tony Schwartz, the authors of *The Power of Full Engagement* keenly noted that it's much better to manage energy than to manage time. Loehr originally noticed this while working with high-end tennis stars. Quality and timing of rest differentiated talented tennis stars who won the big Opens, not technical finesse. For many people, high productivity comes in bursts, depending on how you rest and perform. And more importantly, you can design your work environment for this.

Quality and timing of rest differentiated talented tennis stars who won the big Opens

In a corporate context, you will experience different energy levels throughout the day. Or throughout your productivity cycle. The elapsed allocated time isn't that important; it's often a lagging variable. It's more accurate to assume you will produce an uneven amount of output in any workday. You can particularly see this in intensely creative or analytical work. There might be two or three hours a day where you are at your peak in terms of energy, and you can create a lot of "output". Then, the rest of the day, you'll find it unsustainable to keep going at that pace. You can use that time for everything else when you work in a team: admin work, catching up with other people, providing feedback, or whatever else. The same can be true of longer time periods to a lesser extent. For example, after a period of high stress, the productivity of an entire team can collapse from exhaustion and possibly even burnout.

It's better for the team to define their own workflows based on their energy and availability levels; you'll get better results. This is one of the risks in abstracting and tracking larger pieces of work using spreadsheets. It looks nice to have all the people down one column and then a variable like time allocated or even elapsed across the top. But in fact, it doesn't show how the team works. The output it achieves. The energy levels and how they affect the team dynamics. That needs to be done in another way. All it implies is how you are spending your money.

And in fact, it is these individual energy levels that almost dictate actual output, particularly at different times of day across different people. Team members themselves are best placed to know this–better than anyone who's managing them. You're much better off defining expected output at a team level. Then, allowing the team to figure out the best way to achieve the output goal. You give them the flexibility to achieve the goal however they want. They can work with their biorhythms, personal schedules, and rest cycles without feeling they need to apologize for them.

Agile and Scrum allow teams to optimize for this. Individuals can work when they work best, while still coordinating with teammates. And ultimately, if the agreed output arrives on time and on cadence, there is no need for executives to micro-manage junior employee time.

A useful way to think about tactical use of rest and breaks. When you feel tired, consider which type of break your body and mind need:

1. Minutes: take a 5-minute breather, go meditate, and get physical by taking a short walk.
2. Hours: take the afternoon off if you've been productive that morning or that week and feel tired.
3. Days: schedule regular vacations to recharge, and don't take your laptop with you. Doing this at the beginning of the year ensures that you always have a vacation to look forwards to.

Many people are actually more productive by "sprinting" and then resting, rather than just trying to get into a routine "marathon" where you crank out long stretches of work based on tweaking your life for optimal conditions.

Key Takeaways

- Time does not always equal money linearly, particularly looking through a customer's eyes.
- Three examples of this are:
    1. Work that you can tie directly to customer benefit should be a higher priority than other work.
    2. Tasks themselves can have wildly different "market" values: focus on high-value tasks like unique and valuable $10,000/hr. work, and outsource or delegate downwards as much as you can of the remainder.

3. Output will jump throughout the day. Judiciously using rest will help maximize overall output levels.

Revisiting individual productivity

Once you have this setup, utilization (and output) are put in the right context. At this point, you can track the relationship between utilization and output, down to an individual level.

Once the target output is defined and tied to an outcome, it makes sense to look at individual contribution. Even if you are managing people whose work you don't understand in detail, the social gel of the team will help the team keep one another accountable.

The most effective mindset

In the context of a larger company, continually ask yourself, "How can I make this person's day? How can I help this person feel good about themselves?" Often, asking people respectfully and then digging into their answers will accomplish that. In addition to learning more about what motivates your colleagues, they'll be happy to engage and connect with you. This type of insight feels obvious when you hear about it, i.e. you've seen your grandmother in action doing this for years, yet it's rare in practice-especially in the workplace.

Not coincidentally, it's core to the research of Jane Dutton, author of *Energize your Workplace*. She's done extensive research comparing high and low performing groups at work. At the core, this kind mindset helped individuals engage well, which eventually spilled over into group dynamics.

Influence others by understanding their motivation

In the classic book *Influence without Authority*, Cohen and Bradford argue that motivation will be specific to what each individual values. If you can offer it to them, a 'currency', then you can negotiate your way out of difficult situations at work. The book goes into all kinds of currencies that drive people, which can serve as a jumping off point to get beyond the typical mindset of throwing more money at people so they perform better. If money doesn't motivate them, then it won't change much anyway.

Influence applies to individual productivity also. Something motivates everyone. Put on your Sherlock Holmes thinking cap, and figure out what that troublesome employee isn't getting that they actually want.

Troubleshooting

I've only needed to step in, when I identified that it wasn't working well enough because of a lopsided group dynamic. At that point, you identify any underperformers and work through their challenges using Jonathan Raymond's Accountability Dial mentioned earlier. Also consider psychological safety of the team and that person, to ensure that you are getting an accurate picture of what's happening.

All that being said, there may be good reasons why you manage individuals using traditional approaches to project management:

- If you do a lot of client-facing projects with contractually enforced timelines, then it won't make sense for you to move to an Agile way of working.
- If coordinating across multiple streams and departments, the work is complicated enough that the underlying teams wouldn't be able to handle it themselves.
- If you need to log costs with a lot of precision, and people are a major contributor to those costs, you will probably need some time tracking.

These are legitimate reasons to use traditional project management techniques like Gantt charts. Just be aware of the above caveats about time management.

Key Takeaways

- Once you have a clear picture of outcomes and team level output, then it makes sense to look at individual contribution.

- Jonathan Raymond's accountability dial is a good framework to address performance issues and give feedback.

How to track productivity in real-time

Measures of productivity are unstable in an uncertain environment. Goals-or intended outcomes-can change. In an outcome-based approach, productivity is measured relative to a business goal. It doesn't matter if you are efficient, if you aren't clear and agree on where you are going. So everyone needs to be clear on what the true goal is. Once you've decided on one or more outcomes you're trying to achieve, then it makes sense to track output.

Agile shines at this level. For example, in an Agile environment, this is done first at a higher level with a roadmap of roughly what order certain features or teams expect to work. And each of those items is broken down and estimated more granularly, when needed. If you divide work up into small, discrete, team-level tasks—that are valuable to customers when completed—it's much easier to track team progress. You can divide work up relatively objectively, regardless of who you expect to pick up individual tasks.

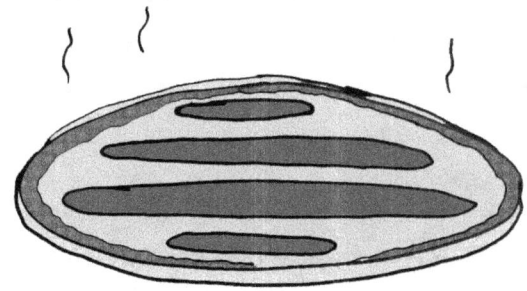

Like project work, if you slice the pepperoni horizontally when starting...

In my opinion, this is the key analytical insight an Agile (or Lean) approach enables. Granularly sliced up and grouped units of work free you up to prioritize, re-order, and manage them effectively-as the situation changes.

Breaking down the work effectively is the first step. When you break down an epically large team mission this way, you get the ability to prioritize which things you do in the moment. Within any given batch of:

- A thousand things that you need to build
- A thousand tasks you need to do
- A thousand features you need to build
- A thousand units you need to ship

They won't be equally valuable, almost always.

There are likely going to be certain items that are going to be more valuable. And ideally, these need to be completed first. With small batches, you have the option to do the most valuable thing first. Valuable as defined by the customer. If your team can't speak directly to customers, you can guess what you expect customers to want. By splitting the work up into small batches, you have much greater flexibility to prioritize. Based on what's needed in the moment, you can tweak your approach.

You can't know everything upfront. Often issues do arise. With this approach, it doesn't matter. As soon as the team finishes the current item, they can address any new high priority that's come up.

There's many heuristics, algorithms, and optimizations for prioritizing so many items which you can apply. This is out of scope for this book. Check Don Reinertsen's book on *The Principles of Product Development Flow* for an innovation approach, and the appendices for tomes that detail the options in other areas. My favorite analogy from Reinertsen's book is that of software operating systems. They are effectively scheduling systems designed to process incoming work of unknown complexity, unknown duration, and unknown moment and frequency of arrival. They queue and prioritize requests algorithmically so well that it's a seamless experience for a child to use a mobile phone. It's possible to extract useful insights from operating system design for organizing work at the team or company level.

As a side effect, aggressively prioritized work forces you to do fewer things of higher priority, and finish them faster. Your resources, time, money, and people are all truly allocated to high-priority things by definition. And you're doing less of them. You avoid starting many things, like trying to run ten different concurrent projects with approximately the same team. Then you have the extra overhead of needing to monitor and keep up with what's where and who's doing what. Most of these tasks aren't as important as one or maybe two. It's much better to focus all resources on that one or those two, fully finish them, and start getting the value from them before starting anything else. You don't become a victim of all the low-priority "weeds". A rather famous example of this was Steve Jobs' return to Apple in 1997. [62]

Small batching is a discipline. It frees you up to say no frequently. Even say no by default. Essentially, you don't want to start anything new until your team completes the current thing, unless there are exceptionally good reasons to do so. You're better off spending more time on finishing things and finishing what you start as a team, before agreeing to pick up something new. Ideally, you want the ratio of starts to finishes to be equal to 1.

Your operational heartbeat

This way of slicing up a big batch of work helps you know what's going on objectively. If there are issues, you have a handful of metrics to guide you. The measure that I discovered that completely blew my mind was called *takt time*, and how it interacts with operational *cycle time* and *lead time*.

---

[62] https://recommendedbyluke.com/returnToApple

Operating metrics that monitor output continuously

This interaction was best illustrated by a bicycle factory in the book *Lean Thinking* by Womack and Jones. Instead of thinking about manufacturing and selling hundreds of bicycles in one go, which creates a lot of coordination overhead between sales and production, it's simpler to reorganize the entire production line to become world class at producing one bicycle at a time.

Let's say a bicycle retailer orders 3000 units for delivery in one 30 day month. There are two approaches. You can try to assemble all 3000 "in parallel", with piles of partially finished work somewhere in your factory, until the last day when you plan (or hope) that you'll have all 3000 units ready. You can fully assemble 100 bikes per day, which works out to 12.5 or effectively 25 fully assembled bikes every 2 hours. If you want to have 12.5 bicycles created in an hour, you would need to deliver one bike every 4m 48 seconds (60/12.5=4.8). This is called takt time. Takt time, the term and the idea, hails originally from Japanese manufacturing. It's a numerical expression of the rate you need to go, in order to satisfy a customer's demand. This can be for an external or internal customer like another department or stakeholder.

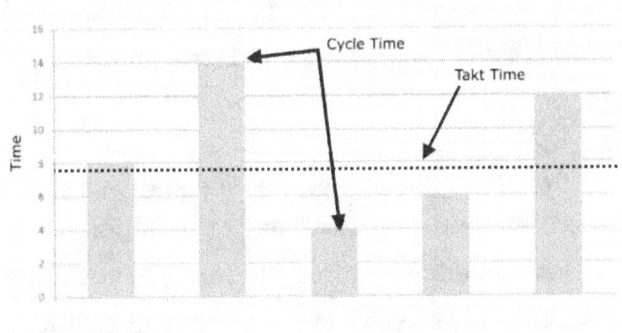

takt time: expected pace to hit a customer-requested outcome

The second approach requires a different layout of machines in the factory and a different way of working, but on the upside it's trivial to observe how many bikes were delivered in the last hour. Or how many minutes it takes to assemble one bike. Calculate how many minutes it takes from start to finish. That is called your *cycle time*. And use that as your measuring stick. Assemble one bicycle at a time. Measure how long it takes. Let's say 10 minutes. And then compare it to your takt time (4m 48s). If needed, optimize that metric. Cycle time gives you an output measure, and the ability to forecast production with much greater accuracy, as you are using currently observed data and minimizing the need for subjective assessments.

Once you know how long it takes to produce one unit, you can also compare the team's lead time to the due date. If you need to produce 3,000 bicycles for an order, and you know it will take 10 minutes per bicycle, then you need 30,000 minutes of production line time. Then you can break 30,000 minutes down across your available time.

Take into account shifts if appropriate. Figure out exactly when you can expect to be done. 30,000 minutes maps to ((30000/24)/8=) 62.5 working days of 8 hours each at your currently observed cycle time.

Using these three numbers, you can figure out if there is a disconnect between customer expectations and team capabilities immediately after you produce your first unit. If you sum up all of your cycle times and add any time needed to process the entire batch, e.g. transport and loading a bike or performing a software release, you get a sense of the *lead time*, i.e. the total amount of time a customer waits from the moment of request to the final delivery of all expected output. If you know the customer expects the order in 30 days and you need a *lead time* of 62.5 working days, then you can immediately escalate the issue rather than taking on the project of assembling all 3000 bikes in parallel and being proven wrong-when you most likely miss the deadline eventually.

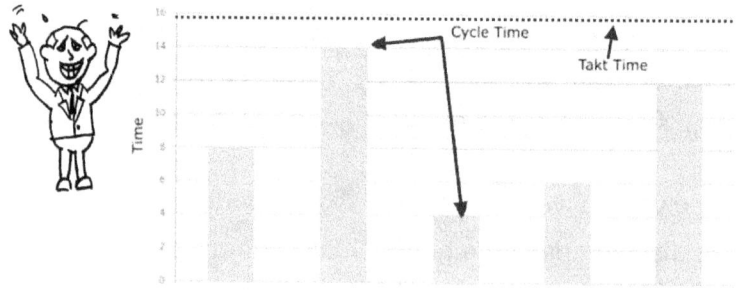

know up front that you can't satisfy demand

At that point, it's too late to escalate the issue. Either

you've got a production problem, your efforts need to be streamlined, team collaboration needs to improve, or your expectations are off, and you need to adjust the takt time to 35, and communicate that to the sales department, management, and customers so you can renegotiate the terms before it's too late.

Cycle time is also a useful measure because it serves as an output heartbeat. Thanks to that, you can continuously monitor your status relative to your takt time. At any given moment, all you need to know from an operational perspective at a top level are the cycle time and takt time.

You don't need more information day-to-day, as you will know immediately if something is wrong. Without creating complicated tracking systems or scheduling recurring meetings, you have created an indicator that immediately notifies you, if something is off. Go analyze, look at it, read tea leaves, do retrospectives, whatever it is you need to do. The indicator merely notifies you when something is wrong. The situation then requires you to step in and collaboratively solve the problem(s). You don't need status meetings any more because the numbers speak for themselves. Instead, you'll probably want to hold alignment or problem-solving meetings. Conveniently, you'll have a crisis, which naturally motivates and focuses everyone.

My team applied the same approach to software development. Instead of bicycles, we shipped features on a new software product. These two monitoring metrics can probably be applied in many industries, if you can make the leap from bicycle manufacturing to enterprise software development. And most importantly, in the context of monitoring team productivity, it gives you an objective yet fair framework to track whether a team is completing work as planned in real-time.

What this means

When you decide to explore a heartbeat approach to operations, you start conversations and form relationships that outlast the initial kickoff meeting. Everyone speaks up about outcomes, productivity, and results. And you identify and clear any conflicts or inconsistencies. During that initial process of migrating over to this style of working, everyone connects what the company wants with the internal motivation of each individual. And these conversations are where you generate true value. After that, you merely ensure the workflow self-sustains.

The heartbeat metric self-manages

It's easier to share ownership of outcomes and achieve more as a group. From a team perspective, that's the most important aspect of a heartbeat metric. As a side effect, activity utilization and attendance-style metrics, which are typically used for monitoring employees, suddenly become irrelevant. It doesn't matter how people are working. If work is getting done, employees earn their autonomy.

If you implement heartbeat metrics effectively, they will be relevant for both remote and in-person teams. And from a practical perspective, this means that the teams connect continuously with the business outcomes.

As a manager, I like this approach. It frees me from micromanaging individuals. There's little need to. I don't want to pick up a notional baseball bat. Beating people up if they aren't doing well. Or use fear to motivate them. That approach is unpleasant for me. It is also ineffective. Gratuitously causing pain and inciting fear isn't a great long-term approach. Better to clear the air with tough conversations. Then reap the benefit—going forward.

Improved group dynamics

In the team-level scheme of things, it doesn't matter, anyway. An integrated team self-manages. Each employee has enough context to contribute. If an obvious pattern of problems emerged with an individual, I would get more involved with disciplining individuals.

"As long as we do it my way, I am 'all in' on this team thing."

Group dynamics become a lot more important.

- Who's working together?
- Who owns what?
- Who's helping whom?
- Who knows what?
- Who can this person ask for help?

Figuring out the escalation points —each person, each type of problem—happens naturally to some extent. Going remote forces you to be more deliberate about it, making it happen and creating a safe space to talk openly about problems. Or to provide and receive help. You can identify experts and organize meetings where experts help. Sometimes that expertise is within the team. Sometimes it's elsewhere in the organization, or possibly even outside of the organization.

Work becomes location, time zone, and time-of-day independent. As long as you're doing work, it'll show up in the team results heartbeat. In the bike factory example, every ten minutes, a bike needs to show up. The team owned how they made that happen. Workers need to be in the factory to make it happen. They know that. You avoid a snappy back-and-forth about availability throughout the day. Instead, you have more meaningful discussions about genuine issues like safety conditions or making sure that front-line employees are safe during a pandemic.

Everyone willingly joins you in achieving company goals because it supports their individual goals. Or if not, they quickly realize they don't fit here. They leave for a company that matches them better. The conversation stays focused on getting things done. And not so much around why Peter needs to pick up their kid and go to the dentist on Wednesday, and whether that is acceptable according to company policies.

Hitting deadlines reliably

That being said, deadlines remain. They serve as key negotiating points between teams and stakeholders. Timelines are useful boundaries. They need to be agreed upon and renegotiated. As the situation evolves, with a heartbeat approach, you can continuously forecast when the work will be done based on the currently observed pace. In fact, it's based on recent actuals of elapsed time (which can't be "massaged" by the politically savvy). It's more trustworthy than other types of forecasts. You have a real-time status, a way of knowing percent completion at the moment. If need be, you can chat with any individual team members or stakeholders. Accountability goes both ways. Negotiate as and when you need to. You've got full transparency, reliable data, and buy in to the overall goal.

 Instead of asking, "how do we know our people are working", be open to rephrasing the question: "how do we know our teams are finishing anything? Can I do anything to help them finish more?"

Even though this rephrase might seem like a wording nuance, it has wide-ranging implications. If followed to its logical conclusion, it frees you up to manage a team independently of their location. People can work wherever they please. Individual contributors have the autonomy to organize their work in line with their natural strengths and preferences.

Key takeaways

- If work is divided up effectively and without unnecessary dependencies, the team can prioritize on the fly.
- Takt time is a numerical expression of demand that the system needs to hit continuously to meet that demand. If current operational metrics aren't hitting that number, then you can extrapolate issues long before they happen.

- By comparing takt time to cycle time, you can identify production, capacity, or operational issues at any moment.

When will the team be *done*?

In team productivity, what matters more than anything else is when the team is done. This is the mind shift you should consider. Traditional productivity monitoring tends to be focused on whether people are busy or look busy. How much work do they actually have? Are they doing it? Do you see them showing signs of working? The assumption is that if they look like they're working for a long time, eventually, they will finish stuff the company wants. In a remote context, it's difficult to monitor if people look like they are working. And with the metrics above, it's irrelevant from a business perspective specifically.

"We're actually done 38 meters after reaching the finish line"

You're much better off agreeing on exactly what "done" means in your context:

- Being clear on expected outcomes
- Agreeing on them with the team
- Focusing the conversation about progress towards those outcomes

Done is a slippery concept. You may lack alignment. Individuals in a group may understand done differently or make incorrect assumptions. Just due to their background, personality, or biases. You also don't know about each role's bonus scheme; your peers may understand "done" differently. As a result, they may try to push you to make different tradeoffs, e.g., cutting corners in terms of quality to get something out the door faster.

With a common definition of done, the shared yardstick is objective. Agreeing on such a definition forces you to discuss tradeoffs as a group. To agree on how to make those tradeoffs. This has both strategic and operational implications. If you have senior management included in the discussion, it'll mean that your definition of done also matches that of senior management, that it takes into account executive preferences. In operational conversations about whether a task is done, the team will hold each other accountable.

If you have sufficient granularity and full buy-in to an agreed definition of done, then you can set up the workflow or production line to have peers review each others' work. This way, everyone gets context-specific feedback on how well they are applying the standard as they complete each piece of work.

It also serves as a framework for performance evaluation if there is a team- or individual-level pattern of not conforming. If the problem exists at a team level, then you can brainstorm with the team how to improve the workflow. If an individual isn't pulling their weight or cutting corners, then it will likely be obvious, even to fellow team members. Anyone can hold this conversation. The ultimate responsibility lies with the team lead if no one else does. It's also an excellent opportunity to re-articulate, contextualize, or apply the team's values to a particular situation when that happens.

You stop the clock on a task, when you're done

You also need to know when you are done, to calculate lead time precisely. To recap, lead time is the full time from when a customer requests something, has the process run its course, and delivers the final result back to the customer (or all customers).

> *Lean from the Trenches* by Henryk Kniberg: "Find out how long it takes to change one single line of code and get it into production." That may well be the single most important metric in a technical project.

Lead time matters significantly more to customers than whether one team member pulls their weight. The time that unfinished work spends in-between steps of a process can significantly exceed any improvement gained by squeezing an individual to work 10% harder. Bottlenecks and work context determine the global system-wide output. Once you remove one bottleneck, it changes the relative importance of each part of the system, and a new bottleneck arises elsewhere. That keeps happening until you achieve a state of continuous flow.

Lead time matters significantly more to customers, than whether or not one team member is pulling their weight.

This is a case of global optimization versus local optimization. At larger companies I've worked with, lead time can be in the months, even for small changes. Because of the number of steps, sign offs, and state gates for a change to occur in the company or in the product. Even if it's one change in a line of code. Lead time objectively summarizes how the overall system is doing and reflects how well it is functioning.

If you're optimized heavily towards efficiency within departments and top-down control, then the space between departments takes relatively more time. By default, nobody will argue the case of work stuck between departments, because they don't see its contribution to the company's overall output. Most people just aren't aware of how important this is, and it's nobody's fault because everyone is acting in line with declared company incentives. This organizational architecture usually has a much bigger quantitative impact on getting things done than what any individual is doing (or not doing).

Key takeaways

- Tracking when work is objectively done will give you the most accurate overall picture of status.
- There are many opportunities to misinterpret done, and ideally, you eliminate as much subjectivity as you can.
- Lead time is an objective measure of how efficient a process is from the perspective that matters most—that of customers.
- Company structure and incentives typically have a much greater impact on results than what one individual does or doesn't do.

What you can do now

The following are common sources of potential ambiguity. When you move to a remote context, you lose natural feedback mechanisms. Disagreements will likely arise along these lines. Therefore, agree on all of the points below—explicitly.

Define Done

Help each team define "done" in their own context. This definition must be shared, unambiguous, and objective. A definition of done can take the form of a checklist. It can also be more elaborate, like a visual. Form doesn't matter; buy-in from everyone does.

Everyone involved needs to agree that this is the team standard, and subjugate themselves to it. Going forwards, the team uses this standard, to establish if a task is done. "Done" is the ultimate state of completing a task—any task type or size. What exactly needs to happen, so that everyone is happy? That definition then becomes your collective baseline. It serves as a rigorous measuring stick for output or productivity, one which anyone can use.

You can also establish analogous definitions of done for any intermediate workflow states, i.e. when is the product ready for quality assurance. Having a clear set of criteria for each intermediate state in a process helps increase the value of visual management systems like kanban boards. The team objectively knows exactly what it means for a task to be "in code review" or "ready for QA".

Team agreements around when you're done

Holding that discussion up-front exposes convenient assumptions and identifies the potential for miscommunication. You can then:

- Apply this definition of done to individual tasks.
- Define done for larger chunks of work, like software releases.
- Define done for individual units of output, like manufacturing a bike.

The difficulty lies in contextualizing your team's definition of done to your team's particular type of work.

This is easiest to achieve in a workshop format, offline or online. You want to front-load the conversation about "done" to remove ambiguity. Organize this as soon as you can. After the workshop, you can track "done" using a visual management system like Kanban or Scrum. Every work item moves left-to-right across a board organized in columns that indicate states. A done column visually indicates what's been done at the far right. You can write up a series of bullet points or checklist items. Publish the checklist for public access by the team and collaborators.

When the stakes are higher due to an impending deadline, the team knows what needs to happen up-front—no subjective wiggle room. If someone wants to cut corners, they will have to get explicit agreement first. If the team has too much work to do to complete the workload according to a rigorous definition of done, you have a planning or a scope creep problem. In this situation, it is easy to jump to conclusions. Don't misinterpret scope creep as an individual or a team performance problem.

Once you agree on a shared standard of done as a team, this standard frames future discussions about work. It feeds into planning and improves accuracy. You'll find it's easier to schedule work, forecast reliable dates, etc. You'll know when the team will deliver certain chunks of work. If everyone defines done the same way, that enables the team to prioritize, self-allocate, and own any number of micro-tasks. If the standard is unambiguous, they can hold each other accountable. They will all know when a task is done according to the agreed standard.

How does the team want to communicate?

Team definitions of done can be part of a larger team charter or contract. Team charters help the team define how it wants to work together. Besides defining done, team charters can cover:

- Which systems store what type of information.
- The purpose of each communication channel for the team, e.g. email for longer form, slack for quick check-ins
- Expected response times for each communication channel
- When each person is available throughout the day, so that team members can collaborate across time zones, define healthy boundaries, and prevent burnout
- How the team will handle vacations and holiday periods to maintain the level of output

These types of discussions help surface the expectations of each team member, in order to articulate a fair set of ground rules that serve everyone and help a team to "gel".

For more practical insight, check out my discussion with Piotr Zagorowski on "How to Baseline Remote Team Culture" on the MRT podcast. [63]

---

[63] Piotr Zagorowski on "How to Baseline Remote Team Culture" on the MRT podcast at https://recommendedbyluke.com/MRTZagorowski

Breaking down and sharing work

Imagine a team member saying, "why doesn't Bob pick up that task? He knows that part of the code the best." If you assume shared team responsibility for completing work, it doesn't matter who picks up and completes a task. It also doesn't matter when the team assigns work. If the same standard of "done" applies to a task, anyone can complete the task. It might make more sense for Bob to pick up something only he can do. It might not. It's up to the team to figure it out.

From the perspective of team progress, clearing bottlenecks matters more than working according to individual specialization. If Bob is currently working on a bottleneck facing the entire team, then it would be best for him to unblock the bottleneck. Someone else can complete lower priority work in parallel, even if it takes that person longer to complete it. The task doesn't need to be in that person's "natural zone of genius". Bottlenecks govern team output. Focus and resources should go to unclogging the most troublesome bottleneck. For the other tasks, it doesn't matter what is done.

As per the commander's intent approach from a previous chapter, it is often best to give the team flexibility with complex or creative work. They should choose who does what and when. The optimal scheduling will change depending on what everyone else on the team is doing when a new task is picked up. This can shift dramatically as the situation evolves. Once someone agrees to pick up a task, she owns that piece. The rest of the team depends on her to finish it quickly. A shared definition of done makes it easier for anyone to jump in and be productive.

There is an art to breaking down work. Granularity matters, depending on your altitude in the organization. If the work breakdown is too granular, it feels like a constant pitter-patter of micro-tasks. It's difficult to see the big picture. The team must immerse themselves in the work to understand each item. There is a complex invisible web of dependencies among the micro-tasks. They all hang together. It may be OK or not. Too much detail can overwhelm senior stakeholders.

Conversely, if work remains large and amorphous, you can't execute. It might not be clear what to do or where to start. It's difficult to make progress if the team feels overwhelmed by external expectations, without a concrete set of decisions rules, tradeoffs, and tasks that they can distribute among themselves. A high level of abstraction is ideal for higher-ups, as they are coordinating work at that higher level. While they don't need details, decision-makers will want to be informed of any details discovered that could shift the big picture. This is particularly common in software settings, where obscure dependencies in software can dictate or overturn delivery plans.

Task breakdown is the critical hard skill

Stepping back a little, breaking down tasks well is **the** critical skill to achieving high team productivity. **Scrum, agile, or Lean management "best practices" don't give you that much in and of themselves. To get something in return, reorganize your team's work-**

load around an output heartbeat.

For example, a handful of delivery managers were running software projects using Scrum in one larger organization. They didn't have a clear sense of progress because the tasks spanned across multiple sprints. Each task had multiple subtasks. In fact, both development and testing staff had dedicated subtask types within each story. If the team needs six to twelve weeks to complete any task—because they're handed off between functions and departments—you will benefit from breaking down the work better. The delivery managers faced stiff organizational pushback when prioritizing task completion over sovereign department interests. The managers escalated the concern high up in the organization. As a result, executives realized that the global priorities and tradeoffs weren't clear. What is more important: speed to completion or resource efficiency (mostly at the individual department level)? For example, it didn't matter how long a particular person worked on a task, if so much time was spent waiting for someone else to pick it up later. Once cleared, the overall speed of output improved significantly.

One last note: if you are struggling to break down tasks, you may be missing or possibly even avoiding a difficult discussion. Organizational culture can inadvertently prevent progress, especially when trying to change how things work. For example, moving to a heartbeat delivery style requires significant changes in workflow. This can trigger resistance to change. If you've identified a bottleneck in how your company works, you need to discuss the full implications of not changing the current approach. Ultimately, you need to create enough space so that you can:

- Break down tasks into small units, so that they are easy to track.
- Help the team ship tasks quickly.

Every company needs to find its unique approach, which will work in its particular context. When you adopt these increasingly common management techniques like Agile or Lean, you can miss the point by avoiding the self-awareness they're designed to provoke. They require courage. If you avoid confronting difficult topics, you end up only going through the motions.

Also, too much detail is overwhelming for senior stakeholders. In that case, heartbeat metrics are the starting point for any status or tracking discussion; well-designed heartbeat metrics map onto strategic outcomes. As a bonus, heartbeat metrics make it easier to diagnose problems together with executives, because you can quantify any challenge the teams face in terms of lead time impact.

Key takeaways

- By helping your team define what done means, you agree on an objective measure that improves accountability at every step of a process.
- Getting into granular detail, and agreeing on what is required for each task and step, helps your team execute and finish work quickly.
- The crucial question is whether teams are finishing anything, not whether they are busy.

Section takeaways

- Breaking down tasks into small team-executable chunks is a critical managerial skill in a remote-first environment.
- At a team level, not all tasks, resources, and even outcomes matter equally when tracking productivity.
- Three examples of this are:
    1. Work which can be directly tied to customer benefit should be higher priority than other work.
    2. Tasks themselves can have wildly different "market" values: focusing on high-value tasks like unique and valuable work at $10,000/hr work, and outsourcing as much as you can of the rest.
    3. Output will jump throughout the day, and judiciously using rest will help maximize overall output levels.
- Tracking when work is objectively done will give you the most accurate overall picture of status.
- Takt time and lead time give you continuously updated measures of progress that function as an operational heartbeat.
- What matters most is when the team will be done. Staying focused just on that is a full-time effort in a larger team.

Epilogue

We've gone through meetings, motivation, and productivity. These are foundational. And if your context switched to remote, suddenly you need to rethink them. Because otherwise, you quickly become your own worst enemy. Your denial can easily become your biggest obstacle to overcome.

If you need a call to action, now is the time for improvement. Just because you survived doesn't mean you need to stay in survival mode. Rethink how you work. Remote is here to stay. Hybrid is here to stay. Not every company will adopt it for the longer term. Not every employee will want to go remote either; employees that do will leave. But there will be a lot more of it, regardless of when we get back to normal.

What may look like a push to remote is a call for more leadership. Be thoughtful, when organizing meetings. Be empathic, when setting team goals together. And be clear, when delegating them. Your employees will love you for it. And you'll have much better results whether or not you are remote.

This book has laid out the basics. Map out your strategy with your team. And figure out how to get going tomorrow.

> If you are interested in having me facilitate your transition online, or help you revisit and redesign it now that you have some experience under these new conditions, please contact me at contact@managingremoteteams.co. I've helped teams in a variety of industries cope with this transition. Ultimately, a book contains a lot of information and generic advice. To make this a reality, you need to transition in the context of your company. Also, you can invite me to facilitate a workshop for your team. Workshops I've run in the past helped companies align around strategy, meaningfully increase productivity, or helped improve company culture.

Also, if you can think of someone in your company who would benefit the most from this book or who enjoys reading books like this one, drop me a line. You may qualify for free copies to gift them yourself on my behalf.

And please open up your local Amazon on your phone or computer and leave a review right now!

Wishing you health, wealth, and aligned teams.

Lukasz Szyrmer

Warsaw, July 2022.

Appendices

Principles, quotes, and rules of thumb

1. Minimize time spent in status meetings, to make sure you can respond to crises and to prevent them proactively: ideally spend no more than 25% of your time in recurring, especially status, meetings (Andy Grove, Intel and Peter Drucker)
2. Before figuring out how to make something efficient, make sure it's effective and worth doing in the first place. (Peter Drucker)
3. Psychological safety enables all participants to say what is on their mind, which is a necessary prerequisite step for alignment. "No one wakes up in the morning excited to go to work and look ignorant, incompetent, or disruptive." (Amy Edmondston)
4. "[Everyone] wants to be heard, to feel valued, and to have meaningful input into the decisions that affect their professional and personal lives." (Moving Beyond Icebreakers by Stanley Pollack and Mary Fusoni)
5. 8 hrs/day is meaningless because of the inequality of productiveness by hour of each person:
    - $10,000/hr work
    - vs $1,000/hr work
    - vs $100/hr work

- vs $10/hr work (Perry Marshall)
6. "Unhealthy peace can be as threatening to human connection as unhealthy conflict. And most of our gatherings suffer from unhealthy peace, not unhealthy conflict." (Priya Parker on the Freakonomics podcast)
7. Autonomy means you don't need managers, but leaders; managers become supporting contributors who help the team coordinate work effectively.
8. Companies have elaborate approaches to budgeting for financial expenditures, but little budgeting for the cost of time spent in meetings.
9. Wolf's Law of Meetings states, "The only important result of a meeting is agreement about next steps."
10. Wolf's Law of Decision Making states, "Major actions are rarely decided by more than four people. If you think a larger meeting you're attending is hammering out a decision, you're probably wrong. Either the decision was agreed to before the meeting began. Or the outcome of the meeting will be modified later when three or four people get together."
11. Energy management trumps time management, especially when working remotely.
12. Team productivity is not the sum of individuals' productivity.

Glossary

BA: Business analyst

definition of done: Criteria agreed by the team for finishing a particular task, regardless of who actually works on it.

department mouthpiece effect: A type of misalignment when heads of departments each make statements that sound good individually, but don't agree with one another.

disagree and commit: rule of thumb for group decision-making and alignment, to help commit to something and start taking action even if not everyone agrees during the meeting

efficiency: how to minimize the use of resources when achieving a goal

effectiveness: concern for ensuring any activity or resource spent achieves the right goal

fireside chat: A type of meeting where an internal company expert is interviewed to share their story or expertise. Similar flow to a podcast episode, and can be done as an internal podcast. Helps communicate that there is significant expertise in the company already.

groupthink: when members of a group avoid raising objections, in order to avoid conflict. Leads to suboptimal outcomes.

high touch: a business based on a close relationship with clients. Often involves significant personalization.

HiPPO: highest paid person's opinion, a type of decision-making bias frequently encountered in hierarchical organizations and which usually leads to suboptimal outcomes because of limited information

hotspot: a point of disagreement or conflict among stakeholders in a company

lead time: from a customer's perspective, how long they need to wait between submitting a request and receiving the end result

median: this is a statistical measure which is similar to an average (mean) but less sensitive to outliers.

QA: Quality assurance

retrospective: a meeting that looks back at what happened on a project, product, or sprint, in order to identify what worked, what could be improved, and how.

results-only work environment/ROWE: {#rowe} originally pioneered at Target in 2002 by Jody Thompson and Cali Ressler. See results-only work environment[64] or gowrowe.com for more information.

single source of truth: A unique digital location where a team agrees to store and process a specific type of

---

[64] https://cultureiq.com/blog/results-only-work-environment-rowe/

information. For example, using Jira for tasks, miro.com for a creative workspace, etc.

sprint: a short-term planning and accountability timebox, where a team plans and executes the next few weeks in a lot of detail. See scrum guide[65] for more details.

standup: a short daily operational meeting used to re-sync and identify blockers to team output. Originally called standup because they were held in-person and standing up. See scrum guide[66] for more details.

status-itis: an excessive focus on having senior leaders being appraised of status, usually resulting in a lot of status meetings and feelings of mistrust

takt time: a measure of demand, expressed as a rate at which production needs to happen, in order to meet existing demand. Originally comes from Japanese manufacturing.

---
[65] https://www.scrumguides.org/index.html
[66] https://www.scrumguides.org/index.html

Bibliography

Meetings

- Digital Body Language by Erica Dhawan
- The Art of Gathering by Priya Parker
- The One Thing by Keller and Papasan
- 7 Habits of Highly Effective People by Stephen Covey
- Leading Successful Change by Cassie Solomon and Greg Shea
- Deep Work by Cal Newport
- Total Leadership by Stuart Friedman
- Games at Work by Mauricio Goldstein
- Where the Action Is by Elise Keith
- 10x Culture by Darren Hait
- Why Managing Sucks And How to Fix It by Jody Thompson and Cali Ressler
- The Surprising Science of Meetings by Steven Rogelberg
- First Ninety Days by Michael Watkins
- 12 by Wagner and Harter of the Gallup Organization
- Peopleware by Tom DeMarco
- Peer Learning Guide by Bart Doorenwert and Salim Virani
- The Culture Code by Daniel Coyle
- Flow by Mihaly Csikszentmihalyi

- Gamestorming by Dave Gray, Sunni Brown, and James Macanufo
- The Surprising Power of Liberating Structures by Henri Lipmanowicz and Keith McCandless
- High Throughput Management by Andy Grove
- The Effective Executive by Peter Drucker
- Moving Beyond Icebreakers by Stanley Pollack and Mary Fusoni

Team motivation

- Sapiens by Yuval Noah Harari
- Sensemaking in Organizations by Karl Weick
- Good to Great by Jim Collins
- "Leadership: The Management of Meaning" Journal of Applied Behavioral Science, 18-257-273. Smirchich and Morgan (1982)
- The Polyvagal Theory by Stephen Porges
- The Art of Explanation by Lee Lefever
- The Leader Lab by Tania Luna and LeeAnn Renninger
- Never Split the Difference by Chris Voss
- The Ask Framework by Carol Stizza
- Power by Jeffrey Pfeffer
- The Culture Map by Erin Meyer
- The End of Average by Todd Rose
- The Person in Context by Yuishi Shoda
- Detox, Declutter, Dominate by Perry Marshall
- Eventstorming by Alberto Brandolini
- Fierce Conversations by Susan Scott

- The Principles of Product Development Flow by Don Reinertsen
- Experience Mapping by James Kalbach
- The Power of Habit by Charles Duhigg
- Right to Left by Mike Burrows
- The Power of Communication by Helio Fred Garcia
- Energize Your Workplace by Jane Dutton
- Influence without Authority by Allan Cohen and David Bradford

Productivity

- 4000 Weeks by Oliver Burkeman
- The Good Authority by Jonathan Raymond
- The Founder's Dilemmas by Noah Wasserman
- Drive by Daniel Pink
- Continuous Discovery Habits by Teresa Torres
- Impact Mapping by Gojko Adzic
- Business Model Generation by Alex Osterwalder and Yves Pingeur
- The Power of Full Engagement by Jim Loehr and Tony Schwartz
- Lean Thinking by James P. Womack and Daniel T. Jones
- Lean from the Trenches by Henryk Kniberg
- The Road Less Stupid by Keith Cunningham

Resources

The following resources were ones that I found the most helpful when organizing or moving my teams online. Most were involved or cited as part of a discussion with other stakeholders and seem to have "landed". In some cases, I found that gifting them was the best approach. There is a mix of free and paid resources, with a focus on quality and relevance.

Books

- High Throughput Management by Andy Grove: classic text with hard-won wisdom in technology, also contains lots of quantitative rules of thumb around how to be effective as a manager
- Gamestorming by Dave Gray, Sunni Brown, and James Macanufo: treasure trove of workshop tools and mindset to energize and focus teams
- The Year without Pants by Scott Berkun: story of the internals of how Automattic, a $bln fully remote company, actually works
- Principles of Product Development Flow by Don Reinertsen: set of principles focused on leadership in new product development
- 12 The Elements of Great Managing by Rodd Wagner and James Harter: covers Gallup's insights from

running the employee engagement survey for many years
- Fearless Change by Linda Rising, Ph.D. and Mary Lynn Manns, Ph.D.
- PeopleWare by Tom DeMarco
- The Power of Full Engagement by James Loehr and Tony Schwartz

Articles

- "One More Time: How Do You Motivate Employees" by Frederik Herzberg in Harvard Business Review (1963)
- Lucid Meetings on meeting types[67]: taxonomy of goals and attributes of most common types of meetings
- Paul Graham's classic Maker's vs Manager's schedule[68] insight
- Cohen, Melissa A.; Rogelberg, Steven G.; Allen, Joseph A.; and Luong, Alexandra, "Meeting Design Characteristics and Attendee Perceptions of Staff/Team Meeting Quality" (2011). Psychology Faculty Publications. Paper 96.
- The Scrum Guide[69] by Jeff Sutherland and Ken Schwaber defines how an agile management process works as well as key terms in a short format

---

[67] https://recommendedbyluke.com/MeetingTypes
[68] https://recommendedbyluke.com/MakerManagerSchedule
[69] https://recommendedbyluke.com/ScrumGuide

Software tools

- miro.com[70] or mural.co[71] as online whiteboards
- Google docs[72] or MS Office online[73] for collaborative editing and creation
    - Slides can be an effective visual collaboration tool
    - Sheets for tabular detail and summaries, with each person responsible for one or a few rows
    - Docs for a wiki-like experience
    - MS Office online tools are behind but slowly catching up in this respect
- asking the team questions
    - mentimeter.com[74]
    - standup.ly[75] to provide custom questions and a way to automate and aggregate listening
- tak-tak boards as a visual tool
- planitpoker.com[76]: free & lightweight tool for estimation of effort around tasks using T-Shirt sizes or story points
- ideaboardz.com[77]: free remote meeting/discussion tool, useful for running #LeanCoffee style meetings or retrospectives

---

[70] https://miro.com
[71] https://mural.co
[72] https://docs.google.com
[73] https://office.com
[74] https://mentimeter.com
[75] https://standup.ly
[76] https://planitpoker.com
[77] https://ideaboardz.com

- mindmeister.com[78]: a collaborative mind-mapping tool

Check out the podcast

Browse on over to https://www.managingremoteteams.co[79] and sign up to get notified when new podcast episodes are released and subscribe to the podcast feed.

Grab the audiobook

Browse over to https://audiobook.managingremoteteams.co. You can buy the upcoming audiobook format of this book if you'd like to listen along.

---

[78] https://mindmeister.com
[79] https://www.managingremoteteams.co

www.ingramcontent.com/pod-product-compliance
Lightning Source LLC
Chambersburg PA
CBHW072044110526
44590CB00018B/3035